In from the Wilderness

In from the Wilderness

She-r-man

with Study Guide

DAVID E. WEEKLEY

WIPF & STOCK · Eugene, Oregon

IN FROM THE WILDERNESS
She-r-man

Wipf & Stock
An Imprint of Wipf and Stock Publishers
199 W. 8th Ave., Suite 3
Eugene, OR 97401
www.wipfandstock.com

ISBN 13: 978-1-60899-544-8

Manufactured in the U.S.A.

Dedicated to the God who created me, and to the ones I love: My beautiful wife, Deborah, our diverse and wonderful family, and the many dear friends and parishioners who share the journey.

Contents

Foreword by Virginia Ramey Mollenkott ix

Acknowledgments xv

Abbreviation xvii

1   Kairos · 1

2   Awakening · 8

3   Another Kind of Physical · 16

4   Unexpected Dangers · 26

5   Into the Wilderness · 33

    Photographs · 44

6   Super-Pastor: A Pastor's Pastor · 58

7   Out of the Closet and Into the Streets · 79

8   Coming Out, Again · 88

9   The Terror of Breaking Silence in the Church · 103

    Addendum: The Little Ease · 112

    Study Guide · 125

    Bibliography · 145

Foreword

As I sit here to write, the United Methodist Church is involved in an ongoing struggle about whether or not to ordain openly, self-honoring and responsible gay men, lesbians, bisexuals, and transgender people. Because I know hundreds of such people who have already been serving for decades in the United Methodist ordained ministry from within their church-required closets, the political struggle seems ironic now that the spotlight has shifted towards the transgender category, because here I am writing a foreword to the story of a transsexual man who has already served United Methodist congregations for twenty-eight wonderful years. Will the church cast him aside after all those years of dedicated and consecrated devotion? Or will it at long last permit people to live openly and honestly as the people God created them to be?

If ever there was a "man for others," that man is David Weekley. Even as he tells his own story, his pastoral concern is constantly present, seeking to provide readers with "positive tools for reflection, creative thinking, and personal healing" (and succeeding!). Then there is the challenge David offers: that we readers might be "moved from condemnation to compassion, from enmity to empathy." And there is the sense of an early life-long vocation, as a little girl stands on her wooden stool and preaches God's love to a congregation of stuffed animals. And there is a heart-breaking faith that God would surely perform a miracle by providing a teenage girl with a penis while she sleeps. Even when life has become almost unbearable by age 16, the girl who became David was still open to a "door of hope" in the form of an English teacher who understood the young transgenderist's dilemma and made the love of learning as safe for her/him as for all of her other students. And there is the school psychologist who hears David's heart and supports her/him through the transition that lies not far in the future. Everybody involved in young adult education should read David's story, if only to catch a glimpse of what can be accomplished through compassionate listening.

It is hard to imagine how David found the energy and courage to transition from female to male while she/he was completing college studies, being delayed by only one semester between the several necessary surgeries. What an astonishing accomplishment! It is described herewith the calm understatement of a person who chose the name *David*. First, *David* means "Beloved of God"—and "God" had always been and will continue to be the source of my hope and strength in life" and second, *David* also means "one who serves God"—and "this has always been my desire."

So when David Weekley receives his Bachelor of Arts degree in Psychology (with honors, no less!), he is celebrating not just graduation, but a transition into wholeness and peace, with an entirely new identity to explore. But in the 1970s there was no internet, no easy access to information, and no support group or transgender community gatherings. This alone is important information for transgender people in the twenty-first century: we need to be reminded of how blessedly fortunate we are to have found one another!

David's experience of seminary and the church makes this story a must-read for concerned seminarians and leaders in every denomination. David discovers, alas, that instead of encouraging spiritual growth, the atmosphere is toxic with "personal egos and professional politics." His isolation is only increased by knowing that somewhere there are colleagues, parishioners, and denominational leaders who would be supportive. But there is no safe way to find out who can be trusted! Hence, David is forced to spend many years in the wilderness of silence, ministering with people without ever knowing whether or not their love would survive if they were to realize his true identity.

In the meantime, David is personally supported through a close relationship with Sharon, who sees him through his sex-reassignment phase; and through marriage to Eileen, who bore them two children with the help of a fertility clinic. I found myself thanking God for the empathetic gifts of these women and especially for Deborah Weekley who, since their marriage in 1996, has traveled with David through his final years in the wilderness and has come in with him into the authentic openness that is God's will for everybody everywhere.

David's significant relationships indicate that as a boy in a girl's body, David has remained consistently heterosexual. So his story illustrates a fact that seems hard for many people to grasp: that gender identity and sexual orientation are in fact two different matters. When transsexuals begin hormone therapy and surgical transitioning, they cannot be sure whether they will emerge as heterosexual, homosexual, bisexual, or asexual. But true to his "man for others" commitment, this heterosexual trans-man has always stood loyally with the lesbian, gay, and bisexual communities, and continues to do so now that he is openly a member of the developing transgender community. For David, it was always a matter of where he could do the most good: as an apparently "normal" white married clergyman advocating justice for everyone or as an openly transgender ordained minister. Once he was convinced that the cause of justice is better served by openness, David immediately began his journey in from the wilderness.

As the pastor of a largely Japanese-American congregation in Portland, Oregon, David makes beautiful use of the Japanese concept *gaman*, meaning "bearing that which is unbearable with patience, grace, and dignity," or in other words "creating goodness and beauty under adverse circumstances." This entire book incarnates *gaman*. Patiently, gracefully, it illustrates how one couple bore the unbearable and transformed ugliness into unexpected loveliness.

At one point in this fascinating spiritual memoir, David refers to the "Holiness Code" in the Book of Leviticus, which forbids male same-sex activity as a confusion of male and female gender roles, just as it forbids other kinds of confusion, such as wearing garments made of several mingled fabrics or for planting several kinds of seeds in a single field. David's reference to the Holiness Code stimulates me to mention the recent outpouring of biblical scholarship concerning gay, lesbian, bisexual, and transgender issues. For instance, in *Plato or Paul? The Origins of Western Homophobia* (The Pilgrim Press, 2009), Theodore Jennings Jr. has shown that the proscriptions of Leviticus were written at a later date than most of the Hebrew Scriptures and may well have been influenced by Plato's final work, the *Laws*, which includes a pagan tirade against same-sex love. It was five hundred years before Plato's later-in-life homophobia began to be adopted by Christians, and more than one thousand years before Christians began to assume that homophobia was an essential aspect of Christian thought. Thus, there is no necessary or essential connection between Christianity and homophobia with all its fear of transgender pollution. We Christians can let go of our homophobia and transphobia, writing them off as the pagan attitudes that they actually are.

Toward the end of his memoir, David pleads for United Methodist Congregations to become Reconciling Congregations. He points out that the congregations who have taken that transitional step have discovered "a heightened sense of excitement" about *all* of their ministries. This makes complete sense to me. Whenever I have mentioned my transgender ("bi-gender") lesbianism at United Methodist and other church conferences, heterosexually married couples have consistently sought me out to help them with their relationship problems. Why? Because having revealed my "secrets," I seem to them someone to whom they can safely reveal their secrets. Only as churches whole-heartedly join in God's ministry of reconciliation can they hope to be safe and exciting places for people of faith to become fully alive.

I congratulate readers who are about to embark on David Weekley's moving story of liberation and authenticity. Bon voyage!

Virginia Ramey Mollenkott, PhD
Professor Emeritus, the William Paterson University
of New Jersey
Author of *Omnigender: A Trans-Religious Approach*,
Sensuous Spirituality: Out from Fundamentalism, and other books

Acknowledgments

MANY PERSONS are due special gratitude for their contribution to my life and well-being over the years. While there are too many to name I wish to give special thanks to some who have proven their understanding and support. I thank my parents and grandparents. I am grateful to Mrs. Anthony and Miss Toolis, who supported me in early childhood. I am ever-indebted to those teachers and other adults who reached out and offered support during my high school years: Tom and Lillian Walker, Dr. William Mahoney, Phyllis Asnien, Sandi Ridella, MaryLou Glass, and Dr. David P. Kramer.

My special thanks to the medical teams at Cleveland Metropolitan Hospital and University Hospital who took the risk to walk with me on an incredible journey, especially Dr. Aaron Billowitz and Dr. Elroy Kursh.

This experience of coming in from the wilderness was only possible with the help of some very special people for whom I am very thankful: Dr. Virginia Mollenkott, Chris Paige, Bishop Cal and Velma McConnell, Christine McFadden, Alton Chung, the Rev. Tara Wilkins, the Rev. April Hall-Cutting, Deborah Maria and the Oregon-Idaho Reconciling United Methodists, Greg Nelson, Ann Craig and GLAAD, Peterson Toscano, Reid Vanderburg, Lauryn Farris, the Rev. Tom Tucker, Nicole Garcia, and the Rev. Jake Kopmeier.

Special thanks and deep gratitude is given to three wonderful women whose technical help, computer skills, and patient friendship truly made this all possible: Winnie Thomas, Jane Brazell, and Tina Marie Todd.

A special expression of gratitude and thanks to my editor, Mr. Michael van Mantgem, for his unceasing encouragement, patience, and expertise.

Abbreviation

LGTBQ—acronym for Lesbian, Gay, Transgender, Bisexual, and
Queer

1

Kairos

*O Lord, you have searched me and known me. You know when I sit
down and when I rise up; you discern my thoughts from far away.
You search out my path and my lying down, and are acquainted with
all my ways . . . For it was you who formed my inward parts; you knit
me together in my mother's womb. I praise you, for I am fearfully and
wonderfully made.*

—From Psalm 139:1–3, 13–14

On Sunday, August 30, 2009, I told my congregation in
Portland, Oregon, and the world that I am a transsexual
man. Wearing the ministerial alb, cross, and stole I have worn
in worship for twenty-eight years, I stood gripping the pulpit as
I looked out at the many faces of people who had known me for
years but never knew this deep part of who I am. I wondered how
they would perceive me as their pastor, friend, and the man they
already knew when I sat down again. Glancing over the pews I
searched the faces of the few people there who already knew what I
was about to say. Gazing into the face of my wife Deborah, I found
strength, support and also saw a hint of anxiety in her eyes as she
smiled up at me. Our youngest son looked expectant, protective,
and nervous. Although he had never said it, I wondered if he
thought things were better left unsaid. I knew he worried about
our safety following the impending revelation I was preparing to
make. One of our daughters, there with a friend, appeared eager
to listen to more of the story she had only recently heard; I did

not know what she had or had not said to the friend accompanying her. I thought of our youngest daughter who was unable to be there and briefly considered what I would say to her later on the phone about all that was already unfolding. I wondered if, and how, these precious relationships might change following this hour. Off to one side sat my District Superintendent, prepared to make an official statement from our bishop following my message. I could not see her face clearly, which seemed symbolic in some way, as I was uncertain of what my supervisors thought about me, or my decision to share this part of my life. The rear of the sanctuary was occupied by journalists and two photographers. We had already met with one journalist who was covering the story, and someone else had contacted *The Oregonian* newspaper because they included a section on Religion and often covered events in the United Methodist Church. Anyone there knew this was not going to be an ordinary Sunday morning service.

The message I prepared was titled, "My Book Report." The title was chosen because nearly everyone present knew I was working on a manuscript and many had asked me what my book was about: now I was about to tell them. I took one final look around, a deep breath and opened my mouth. The room seemed unusually quiet as I began to speak.

I opened with an early childhood memory. It was a simple memory of an ordinary summer day: playing with the other little boys on the street where I lived as a young child. My best friend when I was around four years old was a boy named Gary. His family had bought our old house. We liked playing "cops and robbers" and riding Gary's child-sized, two-wheel bicycle. I did not have such a bicycle, and we practiced trying to ride without training wheels. Looking up briefly from my notes, I saw one of the members of my congregation who had earlier asked about the subject of my book. I had told him it was about my life, my faith journey, and my views about the church. At the time he had responded, "Well that will sell about one hundred copies!" I figured that was what he must be thinking at this point.

I continued, now sharing a painful experience. It was the beginning of kindergarten and entering a school system where I was viewed as "different." My kindergarten teacher was very traditional. She often singled me out on the playground, making me go to where the little girls were playing and leaving the boys and their games. She also tended to treat me harsher in the classroom. She criticized me for the difficulty I had in learning to cut with scissors. I was left-handed, and there were only right-handed scissors in the classroom. And when I spoke out-of-turn, she sent me to stand in the corner. I never saw her treat the other children like that. At age six I could not understand her dislike of me, but over the years I began to notice a pattern when I did not fit into the conventional social role expected of me. Stopping at this point, I took one final look around before I made the statement I knew would change my life, and the life of my family forever. Then I told them: the difference was that while I viewed myself as a little boy, the rest of the world saw me as a little girl.

There were a few gasps, and many stunned expressions as I continued. I saw tears in Deborah's eyes, but also pride and support. One of the elder couples in the congregation to whom I had confided in before that morning looked encouragingly at me, as if to help me continue. I did not want to focus only on these early painful memories, so I moved on to share my early experience of God as a presence in my life. This was the heart of my message, and what I wanted people to remember and, hopefully, find strength in for their own life journeys. I described my reliance upon what I sensed as the close and loving presence of God—a presence I came to associate with Jesus Christ. I shared how this experience and reliance on my faith sustained me through all the difficult years that were to follow, culminating in my call to ministry, my years in seminary, and my twenty-eight years as a United Methodist clergy living in "stealth" waiting for the time I felt led to share my story.

Twenty-eight years is a long, long time to withhold such an important part of a person's life. I had prayed and pondered many, many times over the years about how and when the day and time would arrive. I was tempted to speak out about my life many times before that August morning, but it never felt like *kairos*, like the supreme moment, like God's time. So, years passed. In the meantime, I did all I could as a minister of the gospel to challenge the church's official discriminatory policies towards lesbian, gay, transgender, bisexual, and queer (LGTBQ) people. I helped write legislation, curriculum, and articles challenging the church's official discriminatory policies—policies that stated gay and lesbian people could not be ordained as clergy in my denomination. I also participated in every level of church life possible. I served several congregations as their pastor. I was the dean of many camps, covering many ages from children, youth, and into adulthood. I served as the chairperson of official boards and committees, especially those concerned with social justice. It was my hope that as people came to experience me as a good pastor and a good man, when I finally shared my story it would help move people towards a deeper empathy and understanding of sexual orientation and gender identity. I also hoped that over the years, as more knowledge and history came out regarding LGTBQ people, the church would change long before that August morning when I stood in that pulpit to share my book.

As I moved to the end of my message time seemed to stop. Although my eyes continued looking into the faces of those gathered, I could no longer see individuals. I saw the light streaming in through the stained glass windows at the back of the sanctuary. I was aware of my District Superintendent beginning to stand for her remarks. Finding Deborah's face once more, I saw tears streaming down her face. As I stopped speaking and began moving from the pulpit to my seat the congregation broke into applause. I was shocked. I recall looking out once more, smiling thankfully into the crowd and, finally, sitting down. The remainder of the service was nearly a blur. Following the closing prayers and benediction, I moved into the aisle. People seemed to be coming from all directions. Many, many of those who had gathered embraced me and said they were proud of me and of my courage. Some told me that it did not matter who I am; I was their pastor and they unequivocally loved and supported me. At the back of the sanctuary I tearfully embraced my family before we all moved downstairs for the reception and a time for questions and answers.

As we entered the Fellowship Hall I was astounded at everything that was prepared. It was more like a party than anything else. There was a huge potluck meal, and even a cake! Before sitting down to try to eat anything, I walked with my District Superintendent to the microphone: the Rev. Bonnie Parr-Philipson had planned to serve as the moderator of what we believed would be a lengthy discussion with many questions. I was already emotionally exhausted. However, I welcomed their response—I knew the day was far from over. I had also agreed to a news interview following the service. There had been photographers and members of the press present during and following the service, as well. They had interviewed some of the members of the congregation, and some of the others present during the service. I was moved to hear so many positive comments, even when the reporters attempted to entice them with words such as "shocking," and "secret." As it turned out, following some brief remarks and a few general questions, people seemed more interested in eating and visiting. I was relieved but also somewhat surprised.

I went upstairs once again and into the sanctuary where the reporters had gathered. It was strange to walk back into the now nearly-empty sanctuary and think about all that had happened only an hour earlier. I sat down on a back pew with one journalist to answer questions. A photographer walked around us during the interview, occasionally taking pictures. My wife came into the sanctuary a few moments later. The photographer asked if we would pose together for a few photos and we agreed to do so.

Sitting facing each other in one of the pews we spoke quietly to one another about the morning as the photographs were taken. I told my wife I could hardly wait to go home. She felt the same. We were both exhausted. Finally the reporters ended their interviews. I later learned each had run off to try to get their story onto the online version of their respective newspapers, so they would have the news out first. By this time, it was after three o'clock in the afternoon.

One of the concerns of family and friends, and one which we shared, was the possibility of people coming to our home to verbally or physically confront us. One friend had encouraged us to stay away as long as possible that day. So we stopped for coffee and some time alone on our way home that afternoon. We finally went home at about four thirty that afternoon. Thankfully, everything looked quiet and undisturbed. We entered our home and were just relaxing and changing our clothes when there was a knock at our front door. The outer door was open, and through the screen we saw someone standing there. When Deborah went to see who it was we discovered it was a television news reporter, with a camera crew. We politely but firmly closed the door, telling her we did not wish to talk to anyone else that day. By five o'clock our story was on the local news and traveling through the Internet. What followed was incredible. There were, of course, some hateful comments made online from anonymous people. But there was also a long string of comments made in my defense from members of my congregation, family, and friends. People who cared about us called and encouraged us not to read the hateful things that were said. I tried not to, but I did look at a few comments; there was nothing I had not seen or heard before. Now it was directed at me *and* my family. I was most concerned about my family, and their safety. As a pastor, I was also concerned about the safety of my congregation and the church building itself.

By the next afternoon Deborah and I had compiled a huge notebook of emails from all over the country and the world thanking us for our courage, and for advocating for the rights and humanity of all people. Many, many of these came from people who felt alienated from the church because of their gender identity or sexual orientation. I also received many inquiries from parents and others seeking help for loved ones, including very young children identifying themselves as transgender. During the day many members of the congregation called to see how we were doing after all that had happened. We told them that things were really good, and that it was a relief to be at this point in our journey.

When I stood in the pulpit that August day I never imagined the ordeals that would soon come to pass. But then again, ordeals are nothing new to me; I have been dealing with them as long as I can remember. When I first walked into the Cleveland Metropolitan Hospital in 1972 to meet the group of medical staff who would guide me through this process of becoming my authentic self, I never dreamed or suspected the transition that I was seeking would take a lifetime to complete. But, then again, this is *kairos*, God's perfect time, not mine.

2

Awakening

I WAS twenty-one years old when I first walked into Cleveland Metropolitan Hospital. The place was huge and I had no idea which way to turn. I walked to the long information desk and asked for directions to Social Services. I was going to my first interview and my first medical test as a possible candidate for the hospital's transgender program. The woman at the desk gave me a map and instructions to the particular elevators I needed. I could feel my heart racing as I pushed the elevator button for the seventh floor. I found the door marked Social Services and walked in, only to discover the young woman receptionist was from my high school graduation class. Though she was not someone I knew well, I was still stunned and a little disconcerted to see a familiar face. I simply said, "Hi" and let it go at that. She smiled and said hello to me, we acknowledged we remembered one another from school, and then I sat down to wait.

A few minutes later, one of the inner office doors opened and a small pleasant looking woman greeted me. We moved into her office and I sat down. For the next hour she asked me about my life, especially things like my age, where I lived, and my earliest memories of being different. I was a little nervous as I realized for the first time how tenuous my position was. During that initial interview, I saw that this process could end at any point if the committee decided I was no longer an appropriate candidate. At that moment it seemed that anything could happen, and it all depended upon me.

When the interview ended, I was scheduled for my first medical test. It was an EEG, an electroencephalogram that would measure my brain activity. I was directed to an area of the hospital that looked like a laboratory clinic. When my name was called I entered a small room. There was a hospital gurney for me to lie down on, and next to it was a large machine that would register and read my brain waves for about twenty-five minutes. In order to read them, many wires were attached all over my head and connected to my skull with a type of paste. Once everything was in place the lights were dimmed and I was asked to hold as still as possible. As I lay there my mind drifted to one of the turning points in my life that was invaluable to getting to this point:

Standing four feet eleven inches tall and weighing less than one hundred pounds Miss Phyllis Asnien described herself as, "small but mighty." On that first day of tenth grade English class, Miss Asnien set classroom rules I had never heard before. One rule was that we could not sit in the same seat two days in a row. She had high standards and demanded a great deal of reading and writing. She was the first person in my life to introduce the Bible as literature. She had a love for all the arts, and she introduced styles of music to us as well. She often played classical, jazz, and international folk music. Sometimes she shared current folk music that often focused on social justice issues, playing from artists such as Bob Dylan, Joan Baez, and Pete Seeger. One of the things I liked best about her was that she encouraged creative writing. Through Miss Asnien I discovered people from all eras and cultures, fictional and non-fictional who, for one reason or another, found themselves feeling like outsiders and observers in their world. Excited by these discoveries, I started reading books of all kinds, writing poetry, and playing all types of music. As I began to express my life in creative and positive ways, I stopped acting out my pain in rebellious and isolating ways. I always thank Phyllis

Asnien for opening my mind, and for making the love of learning safe for the first time in my life.

One commitment Miss Asnien made to students was that she would stay after school two or three afternoons during the week to talk about whatever issues or topics students raised. Though I generally kept to myself, her openness and love for the arts intrigued me. And so I found myself walking into her classroom one afternoon. The first time I just listened to the other students. Then I began dropping by the classroom about once a week. One afternoon I ended up there alone. I felt very awkward, and we sat there in silence for quite some time. Finally, looking eye to eye she asked me, "Are you all girl?" I was so stunned I dropped the pencil I was holding. Picking it up off the floor, along with my heart, I returned her direct gaze and said, "No. No I'm not." I did not know how, or even if we understood each other; I only knew that for the first time in my life there was an adult who knew my truth. I was both scared and relieved.

Looking back on that day I realized how young Miss Asnien was, about twenty-seven, and how courageous she was to risk being so honest with me, and for taking on the ups and downs of the relationship that followed. Far from ending the conversation on that afternoon, we continued talking about my gender identity. She allowed me to call her at home and even to visit with a small group of friends on occasion. One day she asked me if I would be willing to meet with the school psychologist, a man named Dr. Kramer. After her assurance that she had met him and believed him to be safe and trustworthy, I agreed to meet him. Two weeks later I was called out of symphonic band rehearsal by one of the school guidance counselors. As I followed her from the room, she told me I was going to meet with Dr. Kramer.

The twenty-five minutes resting on the gurney in the EEG room passed quickly, and I aroused to find myself still thinking about all that had happened, and how I had gotten to this particular point in life. I left the hospital that day with a handful of appointment cards of other members of the treatment team and review committee. I was working at an electronics factory to cover the expenses of attending community college, pay for rent, and save money for medical bills, including the ones incurred from this initial round of tests and interviews. I was tired by the time I returned home, so I sat down on the couch to reflect more about all that had happened and the people who helped me get safely to this place. I thought again about the day I met Dr. Kramer and his ensuing importance in my life.

I followed the guidance counselor to another building. It was the old stately looking house that served as the school district office. Once inside I was greeted by a receptionist who led me down a long narrow hall. We stopped outside a door and she invited me into a small room furnished with a table and two comfortable looking chairs. I sat down on one of the chairs to wait, resting an arm on the table. I hoped my anxiety was not as obvious as I thought it was. I had been reading Edgar Allen Poe's, "The Telltale Heart" at the time, and it seemed to me my heartbeat must be as audible as described in that story. After a few moments, a youngish appearing man wearing a sports coat and tie entered the room. He was about my height and seemed to have a genuinely friendly smile. He introduced himself to me as Dr. Kramer. I told him that Miss Asnien had recommended him to me. He told me he had also spoken with her. We sat in silence for several minutes, and then he asked what I was thinking. I told him I felt like I was in a chess match, looking at the black and white board, trying to decide where next to move. He listened but did not say anything. At some point—a moment that I remember to this day—I told him about how I felt trapped in the wrong body, how I wanted my life to be whole, and how I wanted to be able to live like other people, like my friends. I don't know what I expected, but he listened in such an affirming way that in less than an hour I disclosed my entire life up to that moment. That initial meeting with Dr. Kramer led to several years of support and guidance. I know now he did not really know what to do. He had never had a transgender client before. I know he did the best he could, which was significant. When the school year ended that June, which I knew would affect my meetings with Dr. Kramer, I nearly panicked. I felt like I was being cut adrift, to flounder alone in a wilderness again, a wilderness I had just begun to exit. When I shared this experience with Dr. Kramer, he agreed to meet with me over the summer for a mere two dollars and fifty cents per hour, provided I could find a way across town to get to his office in Shaker Heights, Ohio. This was a long distance but I made the commitment. It was my lifeline.

From the beginning, Dr. Kramer thought it would be good for my parents to be involved, or at least know what I was dealing with. I agreed, especially since I believed they were not completely unaware of my masculine characteristics and behavior. Dr. Kramer sent a letter to them encouraging them to arrange for me to be seen at The Cleveland Clinic for a complete evaluation. I knew it was going to arrive and watched for it every day. When it did arrive, the result was far from what I hoped. Rather than contact the Cleveland Clinic, my parents simply made an appointment for me to talk with our local physician. He was an older doctor, known to be a conservative Catholic, and I had never liked him the few times I had seen him for an illness. The first question he asked when we met was if I had ever been naked in front of girls. Wisely wary, I said no, and that was about the end of the conversation. He did not even check my temperature, let alone talk with me about gender issues. When I left the office he told my parents not to worry.

I found ways throughout that summer to meet with Dr. Kramer. I made the same journey for the next three years. I do not know if I would have survived without the fragile and precious link to hope and a future. (Years after high school and completion of my physical transition, I reconnected briefly with Dr. Kramer. I was glad for the opportunity to thank him personally for all he had done to help me live through such an unbearable time.)

Although I told Dr. Kramer about my gender identity in our first conversation, this is not what we first focused on in our sessions, at least not directly. From our early conversations he had noticed that whenever I wrote the personal pronoun *I*, I always wrote it with a small letter *i*. I told him it was something I picked up from the poet e.e. cummings, who also used the small *i*. Dr. Kramer had also noted I had difficulty beginning a sentence with the personal pronoun *I*. We practiced this for a few weeks: I sat and did my best to overcome the discomfort of beginning a sentence with *I*. But why did I find it uncomfortable? During our conversations I began to understand how the ridicule and messages of rejection from so many peers and adults in my life had left me with feelings of being insecure and unworthy. I had grown to feel like an inexplicable mistake with nowhere to find a sense of purpose, acceptance, or love. As a result, using the *I* seemed too self-important. This period was also during a time when I was studying Buddhism. Buddha's teaching on the abolishing of ego matched my feelings and self-image like a glove. For those three years I considered myself Buddhist, trying my best to practice this philosophy through meditation, yoga, books, and the then little known *East West Journal*.

I lost contact with Dr. Kramer when he left the district and area. I remembered more than once calling him from a pay telephone after a painful encounter with either another student or an adult that left me feeling so depressed I felt nearly suicidal. The conscious awareness of my gender identity, and how it conflicted with the way others saw and responded to me, was often overwhelming. The discomfort it evoked in some of the students and adults at my school was often painfully apparent. I once walked into a study hall class a few minutes late and heard several people laugh at me. The teacher heard it as well but said nothing. During these difficult times, Dr. Kramer went far beyond a typical client-therapist relationship. In many ways he was a mentor to me. He opened his library of stored books, allowing me to borrow and keep many of them. It was from his collection that I first read from the writings of Sigmund Freud, Carl Jung, Erich Fromm, Thomas Mann, André Gide, and many, many others. I found more books, fiction and non-fiction, to help carry me through adolescence.

During high school, I had several crushes on young women. From my perspective this was normal behavior, even though I realized most people seemed unable to understand my paradoxical life. I received various responses from the girls I flirted with in school. Sometimes, as in the case of Nancy, girls sought me out. Many of my peers were perceptive concerning my gender identity, even if they did not openly express it. One example is how I came to be nick-named "Sherman." I was in seventh grade and in an American History class I delivered an oral report on General Sherman's infamous March through Georgia during the Civil War. The next day classmates began calling me Sherman. It never abated or wore off, and over time everyone began calling me Sherman. This was fine with me, for it was a male name and felt much better than my birth name. So I was known by peers, friends, and even adults in the community as Sherman. I even had an identification bracelet made with "Sherman" inscribed on it. I never recognized the irony of this particular name until years later, when, taking the name apart I realized it can be read, "she-r-man." For years my friends, classmates, teachers and other adults appeared to know, consciously or not, how I felt inside. So it did not seem unusual to me when a girl would flirt with me. Most of these experiences were intriguing, exploratory, and relatively short-lived. This is often true in teenage romance, but especially so when the relationship is socially taboo. When the sexual orientation and/or gender expression of one or both partners in a relationship falls outside the lines of what society is willing to embrace or even tolerate, what begins as a positive and potentially romantic relationship can end suddenly and unexpectedly. All it takes sometimes is a few stares from strangers, or even friends, or some whispers as the two of you walk by; social stigma can be too much for some relationships. However, it was through one of these short-lived relationships when I was eighteen and just graduated high school that led to a connection with the physician who became another turning point. This connection was my transition from harboring abstract plans for a "someday" trip abroad for medical treatment to discovering a gender clinic with a medical team in my own country, in my home town. This man would be instrumental in my search for wholeness in life, and self-expression as a human being, as a man, as David.

Dr. Mahoney was impressive looking. He stood at least six feet five inches tall, and weighed well over three hundred pounds. He had unruly dark hair, a matching beard, and a huge smile. I liked him immediately. I had recently bought a Honda motorcycle, so we spent our first meeting talking a lot about bikes and music. He liked all types of music as much as I did, and I was impressed that he was playing a small part in the local theater company's production of *Fiddler on the Roof.* I admired his ability to stand up and speak in public. It was something I could not imagine doing. My years of guarded relationships among a small circle of trusted friends, coupled with rude encounters both with peers and some adults, had left me very introverted and shy. Dr. Mahoney knew some of my story before I met him. We talked about many things, and I found it was a huge relief to realize I now had safe medical care. One day, several months after our first meeting, Dr. Mahoney told me something amazing. He said he had located a doctor in Cleveland who was connected to someone on a review committee and medical team for transgender clients! This committee included a social worker, psychiatrists, psychologists, endocrinologists, urologists, internists, plastic surgeons, and several medical students from the university. I did not say anything for several minutes. Then I thanked Dr. Mahoney very much and left for the day, and what turned out to be nearly two years.

It was amazing to me as I reflected on Dr. Mahoney, Dr. Kramer, and all of the people and circumstances that had brought me to this day. This was the beginning of another part of the journey. I was exhausted but energized by all that had happened during my initial visit to the hospital. I was eager to continue.

3

Another Kind of Physical

My visits to Cleveland Metropolitan Hospital continued, as did my work at the factory to save money. I also attended classes at the local community college. While a more open environment, it was still difficult to interact with people at college, so I did not talk to many other students. I received good grades and was able to obtain several grants and scholarships to help me attend school. I was renting a room in the home of a friend's parents.

One day my friend brought home a visitor from school. I happened to be home and was introduced to a young woman named Sharon. I had experienced crushes before, but this was different. I found in her a person of faith, hope, love—someone with a creative spirit. From the beginning, I was open with her about my gender identity. She listened. Then she shared part of her story with me: her faith, her understanding of life as a Christian, and some of the challenges facing her life. At one point, I shared with her that my faith in God and the Jesus I discovered in the gospels was the only reason I knew that I was still alive.

I was approaching my initial meeting with the full review committee at the hospital. I was terrified the day I went for this meeting. I had no idea what to expect. What I discovered was a meeting attended by most of the people I had already met in my earlier personal interviews. After all of the interviews and tests, both medical and psychological, I was about to hear the results, and their overall opinion. The date was November 28, 1973. I vividly recall taking the elevator to the tenth floor, where the meeting was taking place in a conference room. Sharon went with me, but remained in one of the waiting rooms as I met with the committee. The spokesperson for the group was Dr. Aaron Billowitz, one of the psychiatrists with whom I had met. I liked him and enjoyed the few conversations we had had. I began to go numb as he spoke. He told me the consensus of the committee was that I would continue meeting with him and some of the other physicians for another six months before they would consider surgery. He said they felt that because I was so young, only twenty-two, they did not want to make a mistake. The strongest voice in favor of the delay was from the urologist who would be one of my primary surgeons. He was the one most concerned with my age and the irreversibility of the procedures. The good news was they agreed I would continue with hormone replacement therapy. The other good news was that I was advised to enroll in a private health insurance policy. This was very encouraging because many policies included sex-reassignment surgery as part of their plan, so another major hurdle was overcome.

When I returned home, I wrote about the experience in my journal:

> Went to the hospital today, they say they need more time to know me before making any decisions. What the hell for? I've been waiting all my life; *I know me,* this is what matters. How much longer are people going to keep me in pain? I feel so despaired right now. I don't know if I am going to make it through all this. My world is so bad, so bottom right now . . . The doctors let me down. When will my life ever be hopeful and satisfying? I need so much and feel so empty.

The following evening I added, "I have very short hair now. Does that help? My image is suffering, too. I know it shows on the outside what is happening on the inside. A silver-grey sliver-moon is gently watching my moves. God, are you in the moon? Am I part of it all; where are the answers?"

Despite my initial sense of despair about such a delay, I continued meeting with Dr. Billowitz and a few other members of the medical team. I found my meetings with Dr. Billowitz very helpful.

Once more, I realized how damaged my sense of self-esteem was and how I had felt so long like a victim; it was difficult to change that attitude. We talked about my hope of feeling whole for the first time in my life. I had already chosen my new name and was in the process of changing my legal documents. My friends, family, and co-workers knew me as David. I chose this name after a period of prayer and reflection. I chose it because it defined how I understood my life and what I also hoped for in the future: "beloved of God." Through every twist and turn God had been there and continued being the source of my hope and strength.

Dr. Billowitz gave me the name of an attorney he knew who was willing to meet me and help me with some of the legal procedures for changing my documents to reflect my new official identity. I called him and we arranged an appointment. William Meckler's office was on the ninth floor of a downtown office building. He greeted me cordially, shaking my hand. We sat down and chatted casually about a variety of subjects for a few minutes. Then he said, "You know I don't understand why you want to do this; you seem like an ordinary guy to me." I was dumbfounded! Although Dr. Billowitz had told him I was seeking legal help in changing my documents, he had not told him how I was changing, and he assumed when we met that I was a male transitioning to female. I was happily surprised. I explained the confusion and we both laughed. Then we discussed the practicalities.

After I had gone to court to stand before a judge for the signing of official documents, I began the arduous task of changing all my official records. First I went to my old high school and presented the secretary with official copies of my change of name and gender marker. Although the secretary recognized me and had known me since I was about the age of ten, she did not seem surprised, only curious. I was still a student, now at Cleveland State University, and classes had already started. So I also had to go to every professor to make corrective changes to the class roster. This led to a variety of responses. Most were supportive, a few were uncomfortable, and a few others were hard to read.

Meanwhile, my relationship with Sharon deepened. We continued to share our faith, hope, and love in the best way we knew. We loved celebrating the beauty and diversity of God's creation. We explored from the shores of Lake Erie to the Amish countryside of Pennsylvania on my motorcycle, traveling back country roads. Sometimes we would leave early in the evening, at sunset, and ride all night until we returned to the same beach at sunrise the next morning.

Sharon had graduated from high school and, as our relationship deepened, we decided to live together. We traveled to Koinonia Farm in Americas, Georgia that summer. It is a Christian community founded by Clarence Jordan and the model for the organization today known as "Habitat for Humanity." It was a very good trip, but it was also a little scary. This trip was prior to the effects of hormone replacement therapy. I had to depend upon my natural masculine look and demeanor to navigate in social situations. A trip that entailed driving and camping in the South to visit a farm that had been burned to the ground by the Ku-Klux-Klan was exhilarating, and unnerving. We stayed only a few days, helping with chores and listening to some of the Bible study conversations. But this was long before I felt safe in any kind of Christian community, and I had a difficult time in so close a setting, sharing a common house with other volunteers. It was just too soon. So we returned from our trip a few days earlier than planned. In one of my journals from this time I wrote a poem about this period. The entry is dated November 28, 1974:

> Narrowing my sense of dualism
> Between mind and body-
> A conflict greater in me than ever considered
> By Descartes or Spinoza;
> a-spin-for life I'm
> Reaching out my hands to friendship and love,
> Thinking "Yes" to Being.
> Anticipating Unity,
> Beginning to realize peace deeper than all eyes and roses:
> This is now.

It was a hopeful vision and dream, and one that became reality in more ways than I could imagine when I wrote it. But it is not easy to be with a transgender partner. I know Sharon endured a tremendous amount of stress as I was in the process of transitioning. The earliest days of a transition may be the most difficult of all because there is so much to handle all at once. I had changed jobs, moving from the factory to a security company. As my work and social life changed there were relationships that needed to be addressed, and decisions made, about who to tell and when. There is all the information to read and consider surrounding legal documents and changing old records. On top of things like this, there are the physical changes starting to take place. For example, in my case there was a rather sudden and definite change of voice. I had surely been looking forward to it, and I was ecstatic, but it was also very obvious, noticeable. I was also working out religiously at the gym, and this was beginning to amplify my improved ability to grow muscle. This too was noticeable.

During the early stages of transition, people sometimes appear androgynous, which can lead to uncomfortable public encounters and unsolicited episodes. Sharon's family began to wonder about our apparently exclusive relationship. One sister in particular began asking Sharon very personal questions. Then suddenly, along this twisting road, things became even more threatening: Sharon's mother fell ill and died. The family's growing concern and Sharon's grief increased the pressure on us to break-up. The culminating event took place on Easter Day of 1975. I was home visiting with my family. Sharon was at home with her father and siblings, including some out-of-town siblings who were home for the holiday. We had finally decided to tell both our families that I was in the process of completing all the requirements necessary to be approved for sex-reassignment surgery. I had lived full time as a man for nearly a year and was already in the process of changing legal documents. Our plan was that she would tell her family Saturday evening. She was supposed to call me Easter morning around ten o'clock. As the morning passed into early afternoon and I heard nothing, I grew anxious and worried. Finally, I telephoned her to see what was going on. An older sister answered my call and when I asked to speak with Sharon she refused, telling me they were all still talking. Then she put her father on the phone. He was a local judge, a devout Roman Catholic, and a loving dad. He had known me for a few years, and had always been kind to me. But this time he sounded very different. He told me if I ever tried to contact his daughter again, by phone or any other way, he would kill me. His level of anger and the language he used that day stung and surprised me. Then, he hung up.

When the telephone call ended it was time to eat Easter dinner with my parents and grandfather. I tried to sit at the table with a brave face while I was dying inside. I still remember the festive food sitting untouched on my plate while I tried to make small talk. When they asked where Sharon was I did not know what to say. I know they all knew something was wrong. After a short time, it became too difficult to sit there, so I politely excused myself and went to take a walk so I could pray and think.

Sharon called me the next day and we met secretly to talk. She had previously moved back into her parent's home while I continued my process with the review committee. She and her family were deeply grieving the loss of their mother, and spouse. This new issue added another level of stress. She planned to remain at her parent's house until we knew what the future held. Now, we had to find a way to see each other without her family's knowledge.

For months I looked around me wherever I went, expecting Sharon's father to carry out his threat to end my life. One of my assignments as a security guard was working the swing shift in a downtown department store. Sometimes I left work as late as two o'clock in the morning. When I arrived home, I sometimes literally ran from my car hoping not to encounter Sharon's father waiting to trap me. At the same time, Sharon and I secretly continued to see one another, meeting in many favorite places. Sometimes we were brazen and bold and I would actually turn into her parent's driveway, turning off my headlights, and meet her in her room after work. We were never caught or, at least, not confronted. We decided to move into an apartment together.

Finally, a little more than two years following my first contact with the review committee, everything was falling into order. I had fulfilled all of the steps and requirements for treatment, as suggested in the *Harry Benjamin Standards of Care*. I was living in the world as David. On August 10, 1975, I worked my last day as a security guard. I wrote in my journal:

> Sunday. I am at work at The Higbee Company as a security guard for the last time. I feel relieved and happy to be quitting this job, also have anxiety about finding a new job. Tomorrow I go into the hospital and surgery is Tuesday morning. I have never been in a hospital before, at least not for any type of operation, however, I feel pretty confident that everything will be alright. For three weeks or so I have gone through different stages of fear, excitement, frustration, hope, and impatience concerning the approaching operation. First I had to confront the possibility of dying . . . and death is still frightening to me, perhaps because I have so much more to learn about life in order to better understand death. So I went through a fear of dying phase about the surgery. Then I entered a stage of frustration or impatience, mostly because the doctors kept changing the day of surgery . . . basically I feel excited, looking forward to a wholeness I've never had before between body and mind . . . There are many times I wondered why I've had this conflict. How did it originate, and, why me? I feel it is innate, from before birth and onward, not the result of faulty learning. Some psychologists claim that gender identity conflicts are completely learned early in life, but my personal experience tells me different. Can we say, seriously, that some people are Black, or Asian, left-handed or right because of "early learning experiences?" Of course not, yet at one time or another some have tried to make such claims regarding God's handiwork concerning me! I believe that as the area of sexuality is further explored we will find many subtle determinants within a person's body and spirit that western science has yet to consider.

I checked into Cleveland Metropolitan General Hospital on August 11, 1975. I was twenty-four years old and filled with anticipation and uncertainty. That night prior to surgery I lay awake long into the night, staring out at the night sky from my window, wondering what tomorrow would be like. From my twelfth floor room, everything below looked distant and small. I had a long talk with God that night, finally coming to peace about whatever the future held. Following that prayer I fell asleep. I awakened to nurses checking my vital signs and preparing to inject me with pre-surgical medications. I do not remember much immediately following surgery except the voices of some people encouraging me to breathe deeper, and to wake up. Sharon was exhausted and left after I was back in my room. My parents stopped by for a quick, and only, visit. My mother said it was too difficult for her to see me in pain. I appreciated that they visited me at all, and was grateful for the continued support they offered for the remainder of their lives. I can only imagine the stares and sense of awkwardness they must have faced from some of the staff. The head nurse on the day shift was particularly mean-spirited. Because the legal system and record keeping moved so slowly, the hospital was behind in updating my name. This meant the head nurse could argue that my "old" name be on the headboard of my bed. When I was conscious enough to discover what she had done, I complained. A temporary solution was found by placing only my last name and former first initial on the headboard.

I awoke from surgery around three o'clock in the morning. I was grateful to be awake, and dismayed when a nurse came by with an injection for pain which caused me to fall asleep again.

The next morning, when I needed to use the restroom, the aide simply told me to walk to the bathroom while pushing my I.V. pole. When my surgeon found out about this later, he was furious. I had a skin graft that needed time to heal, and I should not have gotten out of bed. In fact, that was the last time I got out of bed for the next eight days. I spent nearly two weeks in bed, the first eight days with a wire cage around my torso so nothing could touch my body. Eventually, I was slowly allowed to stand and begin walking again. On August 19, eight days following surgery, I wrote: "Today I feel very good about the operation and my new body. I really like it. I am now as I should have been born, almost. After the next surgery I should feel even more complete, yet I feel so good now: I thank God for so much help and love."

Following so long a time in bed, two nurses had to help hold me up the first time I stood. From that dubious stance I began walking the circular hospital floor, pushing my drain and I.V. pole. It felt wonderful to walk again, and I became acquainted with several patients on the floor, though none of them knew why I was there. I was simply "David," a fellow patient to commiserate with mostly about how good it will be to go home. I was continuing to run a low-grade fever, and my surgeon wanted a little more healing of the graft before I was discharged. The hospital Chaplin visited several times during my stay. The Chaplain never asked why I was hospitalized and I do not know if he knew anything about my story. He was interesting to visit with, and recognized the multi-colored robe I received as a gift, and wore every day, as symbolic of Joseph's "robe of many colors." This robe was an interesting symbol, as it has since been described as something like a gown or type of dress a royal princess might wear. In Peterson Toscano's play, *Transfigurations: transgressing gender in the Bible,* he suggests that perhaps Joseph was transgender and/or androgynous in appearance. I knew none of this at the time; I only knew that the Joseph story had always given me a sense of hope and trust in God.

I was discharged on August 27, just sixteen days following my surgery. It was wonderful to leave the hospital, although my sense of exhilaration was tempered with anxiety about post-surgical care instructions and the next surgery, already scheduled to take place in three months.

The three months between surgeries were difficult. It was a critical period of healing for the graft, and it made dressing and doing much physical activity uncomfortable. In addition, I took three baths every day to help the healing process. As it turned out, I missed one semester of college during my senior year between the surgeries. It was too difficult to try to find clothes that comfortably fit, and initially, it was difficult for me to spend long periods of time sitting. Spending most of my time at home for nearly three months, I tried to focus my energy on dietary health and exercise in preparation for the next procedure, coming up in November.

The next surgeries took place at the end of November and then in early December of 1975. While the surgeries went well, the people and situations I sometimes faced in the hospital were more emotionally difficult than I anticipated. By my second hospitalization, I realized how much of a curiosity I was for some people, even some who served as medical staff. There were times I was asked incredibly insensitive questions. One orderly offered to pay me to show him the results of my surgery. In addition, I was so very tired of I.V.s, drains, undergoing anesthesia, and waking up sick. The days of pain and physical recovery were draining as well. When the surgeries were completed, it took a full six months to really feel healed and strong again. I have never been at ease with medical procedures, and all of the physical processes were challenging. If there had been any other way to live my life, believe me, I, of all people, would have found it. In my journal at this time I wrote about the new understanding I felt for people who had to face long-term illness and multiple surgeries.

The autumn following these hospitalizations I graduated from college with honors and with a Bachelor of Arts degree in Psychology. It was September of 1976 and I received my degree as David. Walking across that graduation platform was, in many ways, celebrating more than one graduation and transition. I finally felt whole, at peace with myself, and ready to explore my new life.

4

Unexpected Dangers

THOSE YEARS working with the Review Committee, and those years of being surrounded and supported by a loving partner, solid friends, and trusted professionals, made me strong but left me unprepared for living completely on my own. The stressful and tumultuous years of my transitioning, and family grief and pressures stemming from her mother's death led Sharon and I to separate. I moved into an apartment closer to my work at a small psychiatric hospital. I was planning to enroll in graduate studies in psychology, but I wanted some work experience first. I shared the apartment with another psychology graduate who worked at the same hospital. He knew nothing about my story or surgeries. This was my first exposure to life in the "real" world. In many ways it was like beginning life all over again. I quickly discovered that the new women I met saw me very differently than my women friends who knew my history. On the one hand I felt excluded from the relaxed warmth and intimacy I was accustomed to when viewed as someone of the same sex; on the other hand, I was excited but ill-prepared for social clues regarding attraction, dating, and how to develop a relationship with someone of the opposite sex. There was also the issue of what to do when dating led to desire, which in turn meant I needed a plan for disclosing my history.

I discovered that relationships with new male friends who knew nothing of my story were different, as well. In general, I found that people were less careful of me, and less careful around me. Bonding with same sex friends, and exploring dating with the opposite sex, gave me experiences that had been missing from my life. It was a lot like learning middle-school skills as a young adult, with the additional complication of being transgender in a world where most people had never even heard about people like me. And while I experienced and found this new world exciting, appealing, and exhilarating to explore, I was profoundly aware of my unique perspective and being. I quickly discovered that, with or without my surgeries, my life experience would always be rare, no matter how society saw my gender. Truly, I was at peace for the first time in my life in so many ways, yet I remained a marginal person in so many others. I wrote a poem in the midst of my hospitalizations, in the spring of 1975 in which I attempted to describe this. I titled it, "The Ecstatic":

> Rain spots a puzzled face. In the lake it circles,
> expanding back into the larger body.
> Himself staring intently into space,
> abandoned in sentiments that ache
> enough for some to name him Teacher,
> others, dumb;
> Most name him nothing,
> They don't see
> Him, only the function he
> performs, filling endless maddening demands.
>
> He watches, brutalized
> by all the hardened, empty eyes
> that lodge behind tight lips, impatient hands;
> wondering how those
> features ever froze
> in such deformity; unbending, moving yet unmoved, adrift
> in watches, coats, and rings
> loving only unlovely things.
>
> For most, subtle, social shock is all they feel inside
> Such insulated drives.
> For him, a mental tempest, a Grand Mal seizure of the Self
> When faced with more of nothing else.
> Needing from this casual society
> passionate spontaneity

that most are too narcotized to give.
He cannot explain, there are no controls
Once having opened, he cannot close;
So like a cloud, quiet and cold
He glides slowly through their spacious souls.

I continued to glide. Developing new friendships with men was generally easy, though there were nuances to "natural" behaviors I had to learn. Restroom use and behavior was new territory for me. I had managed to avoid the use of public restrooms for years, even at the cost of physical discomfort, pain, and bladder damage. Unlike most children and youth, I was not gradually socialized in restroom etiquette; I learned it on my own all at once the first time I collected enough courage to push open the Men's Room door on campus. I still recall my heart pounding and breaking into a sweat as I walked through the heavy wooden doors. In less than two minutes, I learned that you do not look or talk to anyone already inside. You do what you came in there to do, and you leave. Restrooms are simply one example. Subtle social cues and knowledge make up a lot of daily human behaviors and interaction, and it is not easy to learn all of this while immersed in the age-appropriate activities of daily life. The degree of emotion to show or not show in any given situation, how long to hold a handshake, or even how hard to grasp another's hand were things I had to guess and work out. What to say or do if I am not really attracted to someone beyond friendship, be it female or male, was also difficult to figure out. What to say or do if I *am* attracted to a woman was a whole new set of learning skills for me to figure out.

I really enjoyed the variety of new male friends I was meeting, but I also noticed that because the most important facet of my life remained unshared I felt alienated from the new people in my life. The locker room, like the public restroom, is yet another ordinary, mundane yet poignant example of reality. From early adulthood I have enjoyed weight training and other activities associated with working out. I regularly used the gyms and fitness facilities available either at the school I attended or in the community in which I lived. Oftentimes I would meet another man to work out or play racquetball with, but when we finished our workout or game I could not enjoy the showers and casual nudity some of my friends enjoyed. I kept a towel close to me, knowing that despite all of the surgery I still looked different if someone looked closely, and I did not want to create problems, lose my new friends, or risk physical attack from other men who felt threatened. This final concern may seem extremely fearful, but I have learned over the years that there are men, and women, who are so personally threatened by unclear gender identity that they become abusive and sometimes violent.

While I enjoyed new relationships with other men, I was taken aback by the changes in my relationships with women, specifically with women who did not know my history. It must sound incredibly naïve, but I was surprised to discover that I was totally socially inept in these new relationships. As a man, I did not know how to develop a relationship with a woman, and I found the distancing and dishonesty frustrating. I did not understand social cues, and I certainly did not know what to do in case any romantic feelings developed. This reality led to an assortment of floundering relationships in terms of friendship or anything deeper. It took years to arrive at some level of comfort in entering into new friendships with anyone, especially women. I struggle with some of this even today.

I believe my early years following transition were most difficult of all. I no longer had any follow-up care or connections with the very people who at one time had taken such extraordinary interest in my life. In the 1970's there was no internet, no easy access to information, and no support communities in place. When I began working with the medical team in Cleveland, Ohio, they adhered to *The Harry Benjamin Standards of Care*. These standards present an outline for how the process of treatment should develop at every stage for a transgender candidate. In the current DSM-4, under the heading, "Diagnostic Nomenclatures," this statement is made regarding transgender people:

"To qualify as a mental disorder, any behavioral pattern must result in a significant disadvantage to the person and cause mental suffering . . . The designation of Gender Identity Disorders is not a license for stigmatization or for the deprivation of gender patients' civil rights. The use of a formal diagnosis is an important step in offering relief, providing health insurance coverage, and generating research to provide more effective future treatments."

I appreciate the statement about a behavior that is disadvantageous to those affected, and which does, indeed, cause a lot of mental suffering. The mental suffering, of course, is not the result of being transgender, but of how our culture *views and deals* with transgender people.

In the 1970s the greater emphasis was on the need for solid, comprehensive care before and throughout all possible medical treatments, including surgery. But I found, for myself and others, follow-up care to be more difficult after completing the medical procedures, especially for individuals who moved away from their support group. It was common to essentially drop care once the physical transformation process was over. Patients were also commonly encouraged to fabricate or conceal their past lives. I was encouraged not to share my identity as a transgender person except in unusual circumstances. As a result, the emotional and social turmoil that came with adjusting to a new life was a reality I handled alone. It is really encouraging for me today to see transgender support groups in so many cities, towns, and campuses.

Referring back to *The Harry Benjamin Standards of Care*, recent data collected from The Netherlands concerning the prevalence of persons on the transsexual end of the gender identity spectrum. The data reveals that there exists a population of approximately 1 in 11,900 males and 1 in 30,400 females who fit into this spectrum. This adds up to a lot of people who need support and community in some unique and specific ways.

Although there was virtually no social networking among transgender people that I knew of back in the 1970s, I did manage to make some meaningful progress on my life journey in the new world I inhabited. I made new male friends and dated some interesting women. It is difficult to say what would have happened had I remained in the secular world. By that day in 1979 when I promised God that I would at least *try* seminary to get it out of my system and see where it may lead, I was beginning to feel solid, authentic, and confident in myself. This authenticity led me to seriously explore religious studies. When I graduated from the university in 1976, I began working in a small psychiatric hospital. As I worked with the patients, it became increasingly clear to me that many suffered from a crisis of meaning and purpose in life. Many of them talked with me about spiritual matters even though this was a secular institution. Over time I became convinced that what people sometimes experience and describe as mental health issues are, at heart, existential and spiritual matters demanding resolution. I had sensed this truth my entire life, and my experience working with individuals in counseling situations confirmed this intuition. While I did not belong or participate in any church, I did view the church to be a place focused on spiritual growth and relationship with God through Jesus Christ. I believed it was a place that supported individuals through worship, prayer, and shared life in community. I thought it was a place that bonded individuals to one another through mutual concern and acts of support, outreach ministry, and genuine interpersonal relationships.

After working at the hospital for two years, I decided to explore religious studies in more depth. At the time I was interested in all types of religious experience and traditions and so I enrolled in a graduate program in the phenomenology of religion at Miami University in Oxford, Ohio. This led to a personal sense of wanting to connect with a faith community, so I began walking around the town looking at the various churches. It was intimidating to think of actually walking into a church for a worship service because the messages I had heard years ago were all negative. As Dr. Mary Tolbert remarks:[1]

> Religion remains one of the major arenas in which ignorance about and hostility toward sexual minorities still dominate many groups. In most cases, LGTBQ people remain abstractions or objects, often portrayed only through the fantasies of the dominant group itself, rather than real people who can speak authoritatively about their own lives. Many faith communities continue doggedly to listen only to the characterization of LGTBQ people proposed by their own heterosexual leaders, assured, it seems, that no religious or spiritual understanding could possibly be found within the gay, lesbian, transgender, bisexual or queer communities themselves. Such an assumption could not be further from the truth.

I knew from personal experience and from my studies that the church was, and is, called to be something very different from this judging, critical, and harsh institution: it was called to represent Jesus Christ, whose gospel proclaims God's love and concern for all people and for creation. And so I determined to try once more to find such a community.

1. Hinnant, *God Comes Out*, viii.

5

Into the Wilderness

WHEN I became a member of the Oxford United Methodist Church in Oxford, Ohio, in 1979, no one knew my identity. And while it may sound naive today, at the time I really did not think it would matter. From my perspective I was a young man exploring Christian community after almost two decades of estrangement. I was eager to meet people and soon joined the choir, where I made a few friends. I enjoyed the community, and I loved singing; it was and remains a spiritual experience of worship for me. I made an appointment to speak with the pastor, and I remember a conversation we had as I explored what it meant to become a member of a congregation, and why it was an important dimension of Christian discipleship. I told him about my childhood spiritual experiences of God's loving presence, and how I used to pretend I was leading worship. We discussed my sense of call to ministry and he asked me to reflect on where God may be leading. In continued conversations it became clear I needed to explore this further. I told him it was confusing to consider the ordained ministry as my vocation because I had not really grown up in the church. I also had been painfully shy for years, largely as the result of so much isolation and ridicule. I said I was an introvert and could not imagine leading public worship services. He responded that if there was *anything else* that he could do in life, he would do it, but that he could not leave the ministry. He said he often wished there was something else he could do. At that time I did not understand all that he meant. I have come to understand it better.

While I was in graduate school I had the opportunity to work at the Wesley Foundation/Campus Ministry Center on campus. Sometimes we had guest visitors from various seminaries. On one occasion a visitor came from Boston University School of Theology. It was one of the seminaries I was interested in, and so I had a conversation with her. Her name was Nancy Richardson, and I liked her energy, her expressed values, and representation of the school. I decided to apply for admission, and a few weeks after submitting my application materials I received a letter of acceptance. I was also given credits for previous graduate studies and a financial package that helped make the move possible. I moved to Boston in August 1980. It was exactly four years from the date of my first surgery. I was twenty-nine years old.

I arrived in Boston without any idea of where I would live. I have moved this way before, but soon discovered a tight housing market with high rents. At first I rented a bedroom in a boarding house in Newton, but it was too far from campus. An Episcopal priest friend knew of an opening in the Student Housing Department for a Head Resident in a small graduate hall on Commonwealth Avenue in Kenmore Square. It provided a small apartment for me only a few blocks from school. It seemed ideal, so I agreed to it, and attended the weeklong orientation. On the first day, I entered the orientation room carrying a cup of coffee in one hand and my backpack in the other. I could not figure out a way to sit down in the folded, theatre-style chairs holding all of this. Then I saw a young woman sitting alone reading, Atlas Shrugged. I asked her if she would please hold my coffee while I sat down, and she agreed. We introduced ourselves and began a conversation. She told me her name was Eileen and that she had attended Boston University as an undergraduate and had returned to attend graduate school. I told her I had never been to Boston before. This initial conversation quickly grew into friendship. We began meeting for meals and spending a lot of time talking about life. Boston was a wonderful city to explore together. We walked and bicycled along the Charles River; we visited museums and historical places of interest. In many ways we were just like any other couple developing a relationship. As our relationship deepened, I knew I needed to share my history. Past experience led me to believe interpersonal relationships could only develop so far without being able to include my personal history. It is such an essential part of who I am. So I decided to tell Eileen. This would be the first time I had told anyone in several years, and I was unsure how to do this. One day after we had been on a picnic and bike ride together I told her my story. I knew that if I were going to be rejected, I wanted to know before our relationship deepened. Eileen responded with an open mind and heart, and we continued dating.

When classes began I was startled by their size. I had moved from a graduate program of seven other students and we met around a conference table for each class. These classes were more like undergraduate school with sometimes thirty or more students. Partly as a result of class size, the format was more lecture than conversational in most of my classes. I was disappointed, partly because I had a concept of seminary as being sacred space, where small groups met together in quiet rooms that reflected the colors of stained glass windows. This was very different. Most of the other students came from United Methodist backgrounds, and some were "P. K.s": Preacher's Kids—having literally grown up in the church. Some had never heard of reading the Bible in anything but a "literal" way, and more than one student experienced a serious crisis of faith and returned home.

Once I adjusted to the size of the classes, I came to appreciate the quality and scholarship of many of the professors. I loved the class in Old Testament theology I took from Dr. Harrell Beck. He had a gift for combining solid scholarship with human experience. And I was eager to learn about the origins of the Old Testament, the history and culture of those times, and how the original languages had been translated in such a variety of ways over the centuries.

It was an honor to attend a class in Christian Social Ethics taught by then professor emeritus Dr. Walter Muelder. I gained much insight about politics and ethics through both his teaching and sharing of personal life experiences. My studies and experience in his class helped solidify my sense of the sacred relationship between social and personal holiness.

There was a truly wonderful, though difficult, class on Methodist History taught by Dr. E. K. Brown. It was in this class I first consciously realized it was no coincidence that I was a United Methodist. I did not know very much about Methodism's founder, John Wesley, either as a person or theologian. In Dr. Brown's class I first learned in depth of the theological idea of "prevenient grace," the reality that God has already blessed you and embraced you. There is nothing you can or need to do to earn this grace. I also learned about Wesley's method for theological reflection, the quadrilateral. *The United Methodist Book of Discipline* asserts that "Wesley believed that the living core of the Christian faith was revealed in Scripture, illumined by tradition, vivified in personal experience, and confirmed by reason. Scripture [however] is primary, revealing the Word of God 'so far as it is necessary for our salvation.'" In Dr. Brown's class we discussed the importance of this balanced approach in theological reflection; we understood reason to include not only personal abilities, but utilizing current knowledge in the sciences and all areas of research. In Dr. Brown's class I discovered the United Methodist understanding that both laypeople and clergy alike share in what is described as "our theological task." This task is the ongoing endeavor to live as Christians in the midst of a complex and ever-changing secular world. Wesley's Quadrilateral is referred to in Methodism as "our theological guidelines," and it was taught to me in seminary as being the primary approach to interpreting the scriptures and finding guidance for the ethical questions and dilemmas faced in daily living.[1]

1. *The United Methodist Book of Discipline*, 76–83.

Before seminary I had always thought I simply happened to walk into a United Methodist church on World Communion Sunday 1979. I thought my experience of feeling "home" could have happened anywhere. I had read a little about John Wesley prior to entering seminary, but when I read his life story and read from his journals I understood this was no accident. For years, since early childhood I had experienced and talked about a sense of personal connection with what I called God. I did not have a picture, only a relationship. As a child, I had loved the stories of Jesus I heard, and so I came to see Jesus as representing this same sense of presence I experienced. His teachings about the love of God and neighbor, and his imagery of God's initial and unconditional love for us, perfectly resonated with my childhood experience. The new term I had learned in seminary that captured and proclaimed essentially this same experience and truth was the one I discovered in Dr. Brown's class: "prevenient grace."

While in seminary I read as much as I could about how Wesley understood God's prevening, or prevenient grace. *The United Methodist Book of Discipline* (2004) defines prevenient grace as ". . . the divine love that surrounds all humanity and precedes any and all of our conscious impulses."

Wesley spoke of his own personal experience of Christ's love and presence during a meeting at Aldersgate: "In the evening I went very unwillingly to a society in Aldersgate Street, where one was reading Luther's preface to the Epistle to the Romans. About a quarter before nine, while the leader was describing the change which God works in the heart through faith in Christ, I felt my heart strangely warmed. I felt I did trust in Christ alone for salvation; and an assurance was given me that He had taken away my sins, even mine, and saved me from the law of sin and death."

Wesley's life was turned around by this experience, and I was amazed by how he lived out this faith experience through his personal and pastoral life, through preaching and through the formation of small groups to meet together for personal growth, prayer, and practical ministry. In Dr. E. K. Brown's United Methodist History class, I also discovered John Wesley's passion for social justice and other early roots of United Methodism. Wesley was incredibly involved in the social issues of his day. He once declared, "There is no holiness but social holiness!" Wesley drove the need to provide for the poor into the hearts of his followers. While at Oxford, he took courses in basic medicine and first aid and then ventured into London during much of his free time to work with the poor, providing medical aid where he could. A small group formed with Wesley, and this group was coined "Methodists" because they were so methodical in living the gospel; they worked hard to provide both regular and first aid education, and to raise money to provide food and clothing for the poor. In the midst of difficult economic times, Wesley introduced interest-free loans to the poor in London, rescuing them from lenders demanding exorbitant interest. Also in response to the poor economy, Wesley and those who followed his precepts devoted themselves to helping the poor find jobs. In a time and place in which many viewed poverty and sickness as an indicator of a persons' worth, Wesley preached God's love for all and, citing the gospel, demanded *unrestricted love* for one's neighbor. Long before the Quakers introduced anti-slavery legislation to Parliament, Wesley was convinced that slavery was an appalling blemish on humankind. These discoveries about the founder of Methodism convinced me it was no mistake I became a United Methodist. These studies also made me certain John Wesley would gladly welcome me into the Christian community that today calls itself the United Methodist Church.

I was enjoying these classes and opportunities, and beginning to feel adjusted to my new environment, when I discovered an underlying current of dis-ease in the school. It was no secret that some of the faculty and students in the school belonged to sexual minorities. The school has a long and proud history of promoting social justice and incorporating Wesley's values of social holiness in its education and practice. There was also a very strong feminist tradition and movement at the school. One reason I chose to attend there was the legacy of people such as Dr. Howard Thurman and Dr. Martin Luther King Jr. and, also, because of the current presence of people such as Elie Wiesel. It was amazing to me to be sharing the same space. But during my time as a student in seminary, these social justice values were not always lifted up or upheld in regards to LGTBQ people. At the same time, some feminists were openly disclaiming the reality and experience of transgender people, saying there was really no such thing as a gender identity separate from sexual orientation. In the news during this time there was the report of a feminist conference that refused to allow male-to-female people to attend, claiming they were not "real women." This atmosphere caused me to wonder if the strong feminist tradition at Boston University School of Theology would be more adversarial than supportive of me. Without even knowing my history, the women students who frequented the Anna Howard Shaw Center seemed more cool than welcoming towards me, so I did not feel I could take the risk of finding support there.

Faculty unrest and low morale was also apparent during those years. The dean of the school of theology was not an inclusive man. Within months of my move to Boston, the woman who had invited me to consider Boston University School of Theology for my seminary education was fired. Rumor quickly spread that an underlying issue was her sexual orientation. Along with several other students, I wrote a letter of complaint, but the decision remained unchanged. Not too long afterwards, one of my favorite professors, Dr. Elizabeth Bettenhausen, was refused tenure. I consider my Systematic Theology class with her one of the best of all my classes. During the semester I took this class, my father passed away. Writing my personal systematic theology for her class at that time was both challenging and healing. Dr. Bettenhausen was both gracious as my professor and supportive as a sister in Christ. Once again, there were rumors she was denied tenure because of her gender and, also, because of questions concerning her sexual orientation. All of these things made my years as a student there stressful, and I was unable to risk sharing my personal journey, which I had hoped to do. Since my days at Boston University School of Theology, things have dramatically changed for the better. But these were difficult years and circumstances for me, as a recently transitioned man trying to learn to explore my call to ministry. So while just beginning seminary, I realized that if I were to attempt to explore such an unfamiliar vocation as the ordained ministry, I would not reveal my history and pray about what to do. I knew I could trust Jesus Christ, but that was as far as I could go. There was simply no way to know who could be trusted and who could not. Far from being welcomed as part of the community, and as a colleague, I would need to live a half-life—a half-hidden life—a life lived in an emotional and spiritual wilderness.

For some reason, the time spent with both the Review Committee (following the Harry Benjamin Standards of Care) and the surgeries left me feeling like I had to catch up. I knew other people who were already well into their vocations and lives by my age, and it seemed so important to not miss anything. I wanted to experience every dimension of life that became available to me. I had hope for marriage, and with Eileen this seemed possible. On the first day of Christmas break in 1980 I telephoned Eileen in Chicago, where she was planning to spend the holiday with friends. I proposed over the phone. She said yes and flew back to Boston the next day. We spent Christmas break together, doing a lot of walking in the snow along city sidewalks, talking about the future. One of the things we talked about was when to marry.

We planned our wedding for the following August. I would have one final year of seminary to complete. We held the wedding in Marsh Chapel at Boston University. I was employed there part time as the evening administrator, and it was a favorite place of mine. I often spent an hour or more sitting alone in the spacious sanctuary. Because I had keys I could also sit in the pipe organ chambers when the university organist, then Dr. Max Miller, would practice. With its rich wooden carvings and beautiful stained glass windows, it was a beautiful setting for our wedding. On the day of our wedding, the "groom's side" held my parents and several friends. The "bride's side" was larger, seating Eileen's parents, several relatives, and friends. The following day we left on a trip up the east coast, through eastern Canada, and to Prince Edward Island. While it was a beautiful trip, I also realized how little we knew one another. By the time a person is thirty, there is a fairly long and meaningful history to unpack with a partner. I discovered this with Eileen, as we journeyed together over the next several years.

During my final year of seminary, we made some important decisions. One of the biggest decisions was where we would live following my graduation. I had always thought I would return to Ohio. Eileen had no interest in moving to Ohio, and the more I thought about it, neither did I. For the first time in my life, I considered it better to begin life in a place new to both of us: free from my geographical and personal history. I was also apprehensive about unexpectedly running into people from my past. I had not really thought about these things before. So we decided to move west. Our decision to move across the country turned out to be both freeing and one more step into the wilderness. There was less risk of running into anyone who previously knew me; but I also lost continuity, and the support of everyone who knew and supported me along my journey.

Of course Eileen knew my history, and some of the challenges I had faced. She also realized how precarious my position was in the United Methodist Church. I had repeatedly read those sections of our Book of Discipline that discussed homosexuality and ordination. There was nothing at all about either transgender people or the concept of gender identity as separate from sexual orientation, or the need for the church to understand both. So I took the leap of faith and was ordained a deacon in June of 1982 as Eileen and I were on our way to Idaho.

I had met with a District Superintendent from the Oregon-Idaho Annual Conference of the United Methodist Church during my last year in seminary. I liked the idea of moving west, and I had always wanted to visit Oregon. I had heard so much about how beautiful a place it was, and how people were protective of their environment. I had also heard that people were open and friendly, and that the pace of life was slower. After living in Boston, a slower pace of life in a place neither of us had been was an appealing adventure. Eileen liked the idea of moving west also. Following much conversation and a lot of personal prayer, I accepted an appointment to two small, rural churches in southeastern Idaho. I have to confess that when I agreed to move to the Oregon-Idaho Conference I expected to go to Oregon. I had never even considered Idaho. When I first received the call asking if I would make this move, I had to consult an encyclopedia to see where Idaho was! I remember there was one small picture on the bottom of the page describing Idaho. It was a photograph containing a blue sky, sage brush, lava rock, and sandy soil. This was turning into more of an adventure than we had imagined! We were actually excited to experience such a vastly different place such as rural Idaho. I do remember feeling a little uneasy about leaving safe medical care. I determined to fly back to Boston for my yearly check-up. Following graduation, we packed as much as we needed to camp our way across the country to this place we had never seen. The remainder of our belongings, mostly books and household goods, would arrive in Shoshone, Idaho, a little before we did, on the back of a moving van.

On our way across the country, we saw incredible places and talked about many things. We never did discuss my transgender history and what that might mean either in the place we were going or for our future, in general. I often thought about it but put it in the back of my mind, wanting to focus on other things: on this new, exciting, and adventurous place in life. In retrospect, I think we both wanted to just live like any other newly married couple setting off together in life. However, from my own background and education I should have remembered the many ways we bring our personal histories into our professional and interpersonal relationships, and if we cannot or do not talk about them, they can hurt, and even destroy, us.

This realization was reconfirmed not long after I had completed my Master of Divinity degree and was ordained. As a new pastor in Idaho, I and another clergyman had attended a conference meeting and decided to go to lunch afterward. Karl had been ordained two years earlier, also lived in Idaho, and was very interested in mission and cultural diversity. I had met his wife some weeks earlier and knew she shared my passion for social justice and the full inclusivity of all persons in the life of the church. I felt safe. Karl seemed open-minded, and he had a good sense of humor. During the course of our meal, I mentioned a derogatory comment about LGTBQ people another colleague had made at the meeting. I was sure Karl would agree with me. But he did not. He agreed with my other colleague instead. When I attempted to talk with him about the origins of sexual orientation and gender identity, he told me there was absolutely no place for LGTBQ people in the church. Then he offered a personal experience from his past—being "addicted" to marijuana—and the "cure" he experienced through the laying on of hands by an evangelist as proof that LGTBQ people should also be "cured." His dismissive attitude and look let me know the matter was settled. This incident drove me further into the wilderness than I had ever been before.

David at about eighteen months of age
in the house he lived in until age four.

Love of music began at an early age.
David playing the banjo at about eight years old.

Fishing at Grandpa Louie's was a favorite respite.
David at age nine.

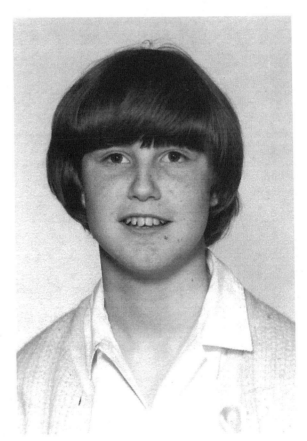

Seventh grade school picture. David with the Beatle haircut he wore for several years. The Beatles and the ensuing
era of social freedom helped make life more tolerable.

Age sixteen. David always wore a blue jean jacket for cover, even on the hottest summer days.

David at twenty playing guitar. He and friend, Scott often played music together. This photo was taken in Lansing, Michigan where they were visiting friends.

Age twenty. David with his beloved motorcycle.
Prior to hormone therapy.

The same blue jean covering, with the emblem of the
karate class David had enrolled in for both self-discipline
and self-protection.

The summer of 1975 at age twenty-five.
The first summer following surgery.
What a sense of freedom, joy, and wholeness!

Standing with Bishop Calvin D. McConnell
following ordination as an elder
in the United Methodist Church in June of 1984.

In 1988 David officiated at the wedding
of Bishop Cal McConnell to Velma Duell,
a member of David's congregation. A conversation prior
to the ceremony.

Preparing Holy Communion during
wedding ceremony with Deborah in 1996.

The summer of 2009. Deborah and David with David's high school art teacher, Sandi Ridella. She was one of those special adults who created a safe and creative place during the turbulent years.

David at the June 2010 Pride Parade.

6

Super-Pastor: A Pastor's Pastor

FOLLOWING LUNCH with Karl and casual conversations with a few other colleagues, I quickly learned that, once again, I was not safe and it was difficult to know who was trustworthy and who was not. Eileen and I had more than enough to keep us busy. Life in rural Idaho was fascinating and challenging. We loved going on hikes and exploring the high desert. I often describe those early years following ordination as being, culturally, as interesting and foreign as living in another country. This new life absorbed all of my time. Between exploring our surroundings, both literally and culturally, and making major life decisions regarding children and future dreams, there was little time for me to think about being transgender. I was too busy. One thing I decided following my lunch with Karl was that, with God's help and guidance, I would become the best pastor anybody had ever known. I made this decision sometime during my second year in Idaho.

My first appointment was to two tiny rural churches in southeastern Idaho. Imagine their surprise when they met me, fresh out of seminary and direct from Boston. I was without a clue about life in this part of the country. Imagine my surprise as I looked out into a life I could never have imagined, and then became part of it for four years.

Under the watchful, bemused, and increasingly friendly eyes of the ranchers, farmers, dairy workers, and assorted professionals such as teachers, physicians, nurses, and assorted government officials I learned how to ride horses, cut cattle, bale hay, milk cows, throw horse shoes, lead campfire sing-a-longs, socialize with other men at the local dump, and do a hundred other things unique to this exceptionally beautiful area. Early each autumn our congregations attended a three-day Family Camp in the Saw Tooth Mountains. I helped out with the program—playing guitar and leading songs, helping with worship, leading some of the games, and occasionally leading a program. I remember one of those weekends when I agreed to participate in a game of horseshoes. I had never thrown horseshoes in my life. I threw six ringers in a row! Louis Couch, who was about ninety-three and one of the eldest people there, had a look of complete astonishment on his face, a kind of grin. I was just as shocked, and I laughed out loud. I have never thrown horseshoes like that again.

Everyone grew gardens and so Eileen and I cleared out a large area behind the church and began to learn about gardening and growing vegetables in this new climate. Many people from both congregations helped. As I became acquainted with these communities, my perspective and concept of pastoral ministry developed and grew as well. We celebrated worship together, shared our holidays, our births, marriages, and deaths. We planned Vacation Bible Schools, summer picnics, Christmas caroling; we offered a simple worship service each month at a local extended care facility. We did so much together. It was a blessing and privilege to live and work with these congregations and communities. There were entire periods of time, sometimes weeks or even months, when I forgot my anxieties of being a transgender man hidden in the wilderness, while living in the literal desert wilderness of Southeastern Idaho.

Eileen and I essentially ignored my transgender identity. At first this worked; we simply wanted to live a "normal" life. It did not take long to discover how conservative a place it was that we lived in, and this increased the silent pressure to bury the past. So whenever I thought about it, I kept my thoughts to myself. Silence and denial sometimes worked for long periods of time; but there was always the annual reminder when the Annual Conference of the United Methodist Church convened, and I found myself once more confronted with my personal history. The scene was the same every year as the Clergy Session assembled. Grabbing a copy of the agenda, I headed for a seat towards the back of the room. I wanted to sit far away from the bishop and the officials representing the Board of Ordained Ministry. In the early years we met in a law school, and it felt much like a courtroom. At my very first Annual Conference session I quickly realized that although I looked and functioned like my colleagues—professionally as a pastor—an invisible, yet palpable, chasm existed between my peers and me. One issue was the near impossibility of knowing who is safe to be open with; sometimes a person can seem like a friend and then suddenly say something that reveals they would not support you, or like you, if they knew this part of your life.

The other side of the chasm was exactly that: the other side. In my experience a transgender person stands on another side, no matter how society defines that side. Many transgender people I have talked with share this same experience of feeling like an observer. One of my biggest adjustments following my surgery and following ordination was to be present and involved in the world, like most other people, and to not feel so much like an outsider. Living in rural Idaho made this easier in some ways because there was so much to explore and do in this foreign place, and I was in a new phase of life both personally, as a husband, and professionally, as a pastor.

Eileen and I had discussed children before our marriage. In high school I had concerns about world population. I always thought if I became a parent it would be through adoption. This issue, combined with my inability to procreate, seemed to make it a moot point. One day not too long after our move to Idaho, Eileen told me she had discovered a fertility clinic at a medical school in Salt Lake City. It was about a four-hour drive. Following a long discussion we agreed we wanted to try to have a child. Family medical history would make pregnancy difficult and high risk for Eileen, and we were not sure it was even possible. Almost three years later, on our final attempt before turning to adoption, Eileen became pregnant. Despite a rough beginning, including one time when we were told Eileen had miscarried when she had not, our son was born the following May. Born on Mother's Day, I immediately ran out to buy flowers, a Mother's Day card, and a Polaroid camera.

Because of my personal experiences growing up, I had anxiety about parenting, wondering if I would know how to help guide my children through socialization when I had missed so much of that myself. But I forgot all of this when our son, and later our daughter, were born. Parenting was, and remains, a deep source of joy. The congregations were thrilled to have a baby in church, and everyone wanted to hold our children when they were small. I know my children grew up in the church sensing the love and support of many adults. I know they also grew up scrutinized more closely than many. Clergy families live under a lot of stress. The 24/7 nature of ordained ministry, the unpredictability of being moved from place to place, the high expectations of some people, and the relatively unstable income of some churches all increase stress in personal relationships.

For me these difficulties are balanced by the joys and fulfillment ordained ministry brings to my life. Even after twenty-eight years I am still awed leading worship, serving Holy Communion, and being present with people during the most significant times of life. The challenge is to balance the joys and privileges with the pressures and stress connected with life in the local church. As a young family we did our best to create such a balance. Between learning how to parent and create a balanced family life and the responsibilities of my two rural parishes, I rarely thought about being a transgender man.

I grew more confident and solid in my calling with each passing year. As I thought less about my personal story, the time never seemed right to share my history with any of my colleagues. Since my lunch with Karl, I had tried once or twice to bring up the topic of gender identity, but I always felt too threatened to pursue it very far at a personal level. So I attempted to educate and advocate for LGTBQ people in the church through my district and conference work. Throughout these years, my prayer remained the same: to become the best pastor possible so that, when I did share my story, it would have a positive impact in helping people to understand that transgender people are like anyone else. All people desire and hope for the same things in life as everyone else—for ourselves and for those we love. Most of us are not media-seekers, and we do not generally try to draw attention to ourselves through extreme behavior, dress, or anything else. Through research and meetings with religious seekers from other cultures, I discovered that transgender people from virtually every era and culture often gravitate towards the spiritual in life. I wondered if perhaps, like me, they know that God is their sustaining presence, grace, and guide.

After four years in Shoshone, Idaho, serving as pastor of the Shoshone and Richfield United Methodist Churches, we moved to Salem, Oregon. This was not an unusual or unexpected move. All clergy in the United Methodist Church itinerate. In my denomination clergy are appointed to a church by a bishop and cabinet, and we are all subject to move on a yearly basis. One idea behind this is that each clergy has specific skills and each congregation has specific needs. So the idea is to match the two, and when skills and/or needs change then the clergy will move to another place where their skills are needed. And so our family moved to Jason Lee United Methodist Church in Salem, Oregon, in June of 1986. This location was another sudden shift in culture, as we had grown accustomed to the relaxed ways of rural Idaho. Our car was broken into the second week we lived there because we left our garage door open. There were adjustments to make. However, we liked being in the state capitol and having access to the many opportunities this provided for community involvement. I continued striving toward my goal of super-pastor. With a small son, and getting to know other parents and their children, I knew I wanted them to grow up in a world where they would be safe to be themselves.

As life settled in, Eileen and I discussed having one more child. This time everything went much easier and we quickly learned Eileen was again pregnant. As with our son, we had no gender preference, just prayers for a healthy child. My prayers were swiftly answered. Following a short labor our daughter was born in January of 1988. For years I have teased her that I never had an opportunity to open the snacks I had brought along this time to the hospital, expecting a longer labor. This time I did not have time to even sit down.

Because my only sibling is almost eight years older than me, I was excited about our children growing up together closer in age. I got a sudden dose of sibling rivalry early on, however, when our son innocently remarked about his four month old sister, "I have a good idea! Why don't we just spin her around and drop her on her head!" Fortunately, things improved over time!

I loved the changes that having children brought into our home. It certainly provided us with a focus and purpose. I loved to play, and also to teach reading using both books and games. It was incredible to watch them learn to talk and express themselves, gaining new abilities, curiosities, and personality traits as they grew. I had a wonderful time playing favorite games from my childhood—like hide-and-seek, and freeze-tag—and playing on playgrounds and going down the slides again, this time with a child on my lap. To enter the world of childhood again through the eyes of a parent is something I would not have wanted to miss. We lived in Salem for five years, and we did a lot of playing and growing there.

Together we did the typical things young American families do. We vacationed in the summer, worked in the pre-school and later public schools, and helped with homework projects; we explored many budding interests like swimming, ballet, wood working, and art. At first with diapers, bottles, and strollers then car-pooling to school, science fair and art projects, and lessons of all kinds, the days passed quickly. In the congregation, the cycle of seasons also continued. We celebrated the seasons in worship, visited in the community, and served on various community boards; we kept up our food bank; and held vigils for peace on the courthouse steps during Lent. The years quickly passed.

Life was very good in many ways. However, on a personal level I was deeply missing a sense of genuine community and intimacy. My relationship with Eileen focused mostly on parenting and work. I knew there were times my unpredictable schedule resulted in unspoken conflict. I began meeting with a counselor in Salem to work on some personal issues. I realized I missed a part of myself that could only be present with people who knew my whole story and wanted to include it in my everyday life. I had been ordained for nearly ten years and struggled as the United Methodist Church appeared to grow increasingly restrictive and negative in its policies towards LGTBQ people. This was painful to observe and attempt to oppose, especially as research and education at many levels in the secular world led to increased understanding of, and interaction with, LGTBQ people and communities. It was also a painful time because by now I had served as pastor of three congregations and lived in two communities where I either knew or heard of families torn apart trying to deal with issues of gender identity or sexual orientation while trying to keep it secret.

While at Jason Lee I continued to serve on community, district, and conference boards and agencies advocating on a host of justice issues, including working for inclusivity. I, and others working on the same issues, hoped to amend our denomination's *Book of Discipline* so LGTBQ people could participate in every dimension of church life, including answering a call to the ordained ministry. I had been around long enough to know there were many gay and lesbian clergy quietly serving in the church under a kind of informal, "Don't ask, don't tell" policy. I did not know if there were any other transgender people. I did not understand how anyone thought this type of silence and denial was healthy or could lead anyone to faith in Christ. I sometimes imagined what it would be like on the day I would finally share who I am as a transgender man, a United Methodist clergy, and a human being. One of the best scenarios I imagined was that people would at first be surprised, but would then begin to realize how baseless the fear, condemnation, and legislative battles were over the inclusion of LGTBQ people in the life of the church. Years later, when I voiced this dream to a retired United Methodist bishop and dear colleague, he looked gloomy and shared that I was not the first person he knew who had tried to keep something as personal as gender identity or sexual orientation quiet over the course of an entire personal lifetime. As we visited and talked about this, I realized that while such a life worked for some it was no longer working for me. The personal cost of silence and trying to be super-pastor at every level was becoming too great.

One place where I found renewal and strength, as I wrestled with my personal life and my denomination's increasingly contracted view and understanding of LGTBQ people, was our church camping program. For several years I provided leadership for many family, children, and youth camps. I learned how to play many beloved campfire songs on my guitar, and had the opportunity to watch strong bonds of friendship form during the five days at a Christian camp where people of all ages shared their deeper selves and openly discussed their faith. It is a powerful experience to be outdoors around a fire and singing to God into a night sky filled with stars. More than once, I thought about how much more I could offer about my faith had I felt free to share my whole story. Once again I realized that one of the saddest ironies of the church is that the very community created for declaring trust in God and genuine care for one another has become a place of hiding for some and ruthless intimidation for others—not only for LGTBQ people, but for *all* people. Because when it is not safe to talk about everything, it soon becomes unsafe to talk about anything.

Looking back, it is amazing to me that I was able to interact as comfortably as I did with many different types and ages of people.

I had grown up with such a unique and very different perspective. Early in my life these differences appeared and often functioned as a hindrance. But as an adult and as a pastor, I discovered my unique perspective often served as a bridge when relating to different types of people. Regardless of the congregational setting or local culture, parishioners over the years have appeared to relate easily to me. Differing views on politics, lifestyle choice, and yes, even religion, rarely interfered in my relationships. I have wondered if this is because transgender people, standing outside the norm as we do, offer a distinct perspective and the ability to empathize with different types of people. This ability seemed to help as I served on the conference board of Church and Society of the United Methodist Church as well. As the Chairperson of the Division of Christian Social Concerns, I enjoyed my involvement in helping to create ministries and policies that affected people's lives in practical and positive ways. We addressed issues concerning LGTBQ people, we advocated for peace and justice, and we campaigned for good stewardship of earth's resources. These are just a few examples of the types of things we focused on. One of the concrete resources we produced was a comprehensive reference manual addressing domestic violence that included community resources for every county and the state of Oregon agencies, as well. On this board I met people with whom I shared common interests, and it became a group of people with whom I looked forward to getting together. I served on this board for several years. Over time my concern began to grow as I watched people on the board drift away. When they left, they generally left not only The Board of Church and Society, but also the United Methodist Church as a denomination. Many times these resignations were from the clergy and laity from whom I felt the most support. I watched the same attrition happen in the pews of local churches as members moved away, resigned over issues, or died. It was clear the denomination was becoming increasingly polarized around gender identity, sexual orientation and other key issues, and losing members on both ends.

While I chaired the Division of Christian Social Concerns, which is a part of The Board of Church and Society, we invited a gay man, Dick, to become a member—the first invitation from this board to an openly gay individual. He agreed, and worked with us many years. Years before I met him, he had been forced to resign from active ministry when he shared his sexual orientation. As we worked together we became good friends, and I regretted the years he did not know my story because I knew there would be so much more to talk about, and at a different level, than when I was simply seen as just another heterosexual white male ally. During this time, one question I continued asking myself was if I were still being the most effective by remaining in this silent wilderness or if I could accomplish more good by openly engaging with my denomination as an ordained transgender clergyman. As I continued to observe people leave under duress or despair I decided to remain quiet for the time being so I could continue advocating for positive change within the system. I thought I could use whatever power I possessed as a white male clergy to help create change, even though, ironically, I was sometimes told I could not really understand issues relating to bigotry and intolerance because of my position of power!

While I was the pastor of Jason Lee United Methodist Church in Salem, Oregon our church hosted a series of panel discussions concerning LGTBQ people. We invited speakers from the medical, mental health, and ecumenical faith communities. We also invited three openly gay men to participate. The series was well received, and the congregation learned a lot, but from a few comments and responses I realized that as progressive and inclusive as the members of the congregation seemed to be, they were neither ready to officially become a Reconciling Congregation, nor were they ready to know they already had a transgender pastor. Once again I set aside any thoughts of sharing my story. With two very young children at home, it seemed prudent for our family as well. In many ways my years in Salem were, as Dickens says, the best of times and the worst of times. I enjoyed serving as pastor of the congregation and I was also involved in the larger community. As years passed, however, one issue continued to reemerge. This was the well being of my family, more specifically, between Eileen and I. Tension arose concerning my salary, and the neighborhood in which the parsonage and church were located. Although I made the average salary for clergy in similar settings in my conference, our conference was the lowest paying annual conference in the country. At the same time, the neighborhood in which we were located was one of the worst in Salem, in terms of low income and high crime. When we first moved to the area, we discovered our neighborhood unwillingly hosted the weekend car-cruising strip. Neighbors had found young adults defecating and urinating on their property. I became accustomed to Monday morning searches of our parking lot to recover used hypodermic needles and condoms. The noise level kept us up until early morning every Friday and Saturday night. One of my first attempts at community organizing led to a successful grass-roots campaign to have a "no cruising zone" ordinance passed for our neighborhood. But the neighborhood became increasingly unsafe. These issues began to affect our marriage. Under growing discontent and apprehension regarding the safety of our children, I asked to move from Jason Lee United Methodist Church after five years of ministry.

The following July 1, in the summer of 1991, I was appointed associate pastor of First Corvallis United Methodist Church in Corvallis, Oregon. I was feeling increasingly alone and isolated on a personal level. I was encouraged when I discovered my new congregation was already engaged in a study on human sexuality and the current position of our denomination concerning LGTBQ people. I began meeting with this group regularly. Eventually we moved toward the position where asking for a congregational vote on whether or not to become an official Reconciling Congregation was the appropriate thing to do. This was a big step to consider, but we had completed a lot of education and conversation. We were also one of the largest congregations in our area, and we felt it was an important step to consider. There were three of us serving the congregation in some ministerial capacity. We were all white men. The senior pastor was hesitant, understandably not wanting to risk splitting the congregation. The campus pastor had helped initiate the study, knew some of the people better than I, and was more positive about the outcome of a formal vote. I was the newest member and colleague, but I also felt positive about a vote. It was actually the laity that pushed us to a formal vote, however. Reasoning that we had completed all the study process possible, the lay members of the group felt it was time to see where we stood as a congregation We decided to poll the congregation on becoming an official Reconciling Congregation following a Sunday worship service in September of 1992. From a congregation of more than eight hundred official members there were few dissenting votes. One family left the church temporarily but eventually returned. It was a great privilege to be the person to preach the sermon that morning.

The sermon was titled, "The Little Ease" and it began with a memory from my own life, but nobody there knew that. It was exhilarating to be able to openly speak from the pulpit some truth from that part of my life. Every clergyperson prays that truth is proclaimed. There were moments when it was difficult not to come to tears. I think that in some way things were never the same again for me after that morning. The initial experience of speaking some part of my story publicly, and from the pulpit, reopened the issue of how long to remain silent. It seemed to me that trying to be super-pastor was no longer working. At the time, I had no idea where this awareness would lead.

Less than one year after preaching "The Little Ease," and celebrating the Corvallis congregation's decision to become a Reconciling Congregation, I was unexpectedly moved. This was a move that involved all three clergy associated with that congregation. As is often the case when the senior pastor moves, all the clergy moved. I never knew if my activism played a part in the decision to move me from Corvallis. I did know there was a district superintendent returning to local church ministry who the cabinet wanted to send to Corvallis, with his spouse, to serve as Associate. Regardless, this was the first time I had been forced to make a move when I did not want to move. The upward momentum I had experienced for two years in that progressive congregation came crashing down when I was sent to a far more conservative and parochial community in Forest Grove, Oregon. Some of the members of that congregation knew my reputation for social justice ministry, including my thoughts about the full inclusion of LGTBQ people. Many found it a negative rather than positive aspect of my ministry. One couple openly questioned me about this, stating they hoped I would not try to bring discussion about sexual orientation and gender identity to *their* church.

In addition to the shock I experienced as the new pastor of a more conservative and sluggish congregation, the move also adversely affected my marriage and family life. Over the years our marriage, that began in friendship and hopes for increased intimacy, increased in distance instead. Eileen had to change jobs. Our children entered into a far less progressive school district. While we had experienced some marital problems over the years, the move to Forest Grove seemed to amplify all of them. While the move entailed a small increase in salary, finances continued to be a sore spot in our marriage as the children grew and demands increased. Though we rarely discussed it, the expectations and assumptions placed upon a clergy's spouse, especially a wife, increase the pressures and stress in the marriage. Eileen had never signed up for the church, or to volunteer in the church; she did so just because of me. At the same time, never discussing my personal life as a transgender man and ordained clergy became less tolerable to me. I began to think more about the possible positive benefits, both personally and for others, to which sharing my story might lead. All of these factors had a significant impact upon our marriage. For many reasons, the distance between us continued to grow.

Our children began to adjust fairly quickly to Forest Grove. They met friends in the neighborhood and among other children at church. They liked living in a larger house. But Eileen and I continued to experience stress and difficulties with communication. Sometimes I thought of myself as a ghost walking through our home; it seemed nobody really saw me. Some of the church members seemed nice, but distant and superficial. A former pastor, now retired, stayed in the church and kept a small group of loyal followers; they continued to regard him as their pastor, creating dissonance and conflict within the church leadership. Unlike Corvallis, I was not invited to serve on any community boards or agencies either. At every level I began to feel unseen, unwanted, and unappreciated. Once again, I sought out a counselor who helped with some issues for a time. But nothing seemed able to improve my relationship with Eileen who seemed unhappy and dissatisfied with our life. We loved our children, but I began to worry about their exposure to what increasingly seemed like an unhappy marriage. I believed both of us wanted our children to grow up in an atmosphere of healthy and loving relationships, and our home was feeling less and less like this type of environment. Despite these things, or perhaps because of them, I was certain I did not want to further upset our family by disclosing my story. I determined it was best not to say anything until at least they had graduated from high school.

At that time, one way I attempted to express human relationships to my children was through the writings of Martin Buber. I wanted my children to know the difference between what Martin Buber describes as "I-It" and "I-Thou" relationships.[1] I had not read Buber's classic book for years, but I found myself reflecting upon it again and trying to rephrase some of his ideas in language young children could understand.

Twentieth-century Jewish theologian and philosopher Martin Buber rediscovered the eighteenth-century Hasidic mystical tradi-

---

1. Buber, *I and Thou*, 6–10.

tion and its teaching that the fundamental commandment in life is to be "humanly holy." In *I and Thou,* which Buber based upon both personal experience and this mystical tradition, he describes an "I-Thou" relationship as any authentic encounter characterized by empathy, attentiveness, and the recognition and honoring of the uniqueness of the other. As Olive Elaine Hinnant notes in her book, *God Comes Out,* the experience that led Martin Buber to this theological understanding was a personal encounter. As a new professor, Buber was visited by a young student unknown to him. Buber was cordial but, as he said of himself, was "not being there" in spirit. Following their conversation the young man departed, and Martin Buber later learned the young man had committed suicide hours later. Following this experience Buber vowed to never again neglect this empathetic form of knowing and relating to another person. This empathetic attentiveness is the type of relationship Buber termed, "I-Thou." My reading of the gospel tells me Buber is correct: this is certainly the way others should be viewed and treated. Sadly, too often this is not the case. For example, even among other minorities, LGTBQ people are often the most devalued of all, and within the lesbian, gay, bisexual, and queer communities, transgender persons are sometimes unwelcome and misunderstood.

Once, following a World Communion Sunday sermon in which I spoke of God's love for all persons through Jesus Christ and openly advocated for marriage equality, I received a threatening email from a man who professed to be a Christian. He said he was a visitor who happened to be in church that morning. I did not know if this statement was true: I had not noticed any visitors that morning. But whoever he was, he clearly had no concept of "I-Thou" relationships or Christ's inclusive care for all people. He quickly proclaimed God's hate for me. Unfortunately this is exactly what so many LGTBQ people, who are alienated from or outside the church for other reasons, hear (while too many Christians who would disagree with this negative message remain silent and complacent). The end result is that all Christians are viewed as bigoted, hypocritical, and dangerous—not only by members of the LGTBQ community, but by many progressive, community-minded people who do not attend church.

Reading Martin Buber again, and talking with a counselor, helped my relationship with Eileen, but it was not enough to improve or sustain our marriage. When I openly shared my feelings with her, she did not really seem surprised. We did attempt going to marriage counseling together, but it seemed that too much had built up during the silence of the passing years. We seemed unable to address and heal the wounds we had buried and borne silently together, and our marriage ended while we were in Forest Grove. While our divorce was amicable at first, over time we grew even more distant. We rarely communicate today.

The divorce rate in clergy families is high. Looking back over those years, I realize how much stress and loss of intimacy resulted from the mutual silence Eileen and I shared around transgender issues, my personal story, and other concerns as well. Eileen and I seemed unable to surmount some issues, and differences in our personalities and interests seemed to increase over the years.

It was difficult and foreign to return home to an empty house every day. But this time alone proved to be the beginning of a time of healing and growth, ultimately making me a better parent, pastor, and person. This was an uneasy time for my congregation. It is difficult when family members or good friends divorce, but for someone's pastor to go through divorce is, for some, too much. I had agreed to stay for another year and ended up staying for two, but the divorce was hard for some of them to understand.

It was also not easy to live away from my kids, and I enjoyed having extended time with them whenever possible. As the divorce altered the routine and arrangement of our family, there were many adjustments in the beginning, and many emotions for all of us to work through. I continued to meet with my counselor and also with a spiritual director. I felt a need to evaluate my life, my ministry, and where I felt led to move into the future. I spent hours in meditation and prayer seeking direction and guidance for my life. Living hidden as a transgender man and pastor in local church ministry was wearing on me, and I was no longer certain that silently working within the system was either the best or most effective way to continue.

During those years I watched my denomination's conversations around LGTBQ issues turn increasingly negative and discriminatory. For some of my colleagues it was unbearable, and they left seeking a more inclusive denomination. For years I remained horrified at the attitudes revealed and accusations made towards gay and lesbian people during our Annual Conference sessions. The level of emotion expressed in debates over anything that had to do with what was then simply called homosexuality made the floor of annual conference an unsafe atmosphere in which to speak. I remember one session where a woman serving as a laity member from her local church stood and, in tears, told all of us how much she loved and admired her lesbian daughter, and how broken-hearted she was by the policies and practices of her church. As I listened to her at that moment, I was both more determined to work within the denomination for change, and acutely aware of how precarious my position was in the church.

The role of super-pastor was beginning to unravel both personally and professionally. I knew inside it was time to make some decisions and changes in my life, decisions and changes that would involve sharing my personal story. I had no idea how or when this would happen. I was initially unaware of the change in direction when it did occur, but as I reassembled my life in Forest Grove I had already slowly begun the long journey that would lead me in from the wilderness.

I met Deborah twice, the first time unknowingly. I was at an Oregon hot springs with my family. I had loved the hot springs in Idaho and missed them; so when I heard there was a hot springs not too far from Salem, we decided to go for a weekend. When we arrived, there was a large group meeting there the same weekend. I was disappointed because it was more crowded than I had hoped, but then I was *really* disappointed when I learned that clothing was optional at all of the hot springs pools. Needless to say, there was not much I felt comfortable doing there, except going to the dining hall for meals and visiting the small interfaith chapel. I really missed the hot springs, which was the reason we planned the trip in the first place. I kept looking at the steam house. It was a small wooden structure that hung over a large hot pool. The steam from the pool entered the steam house. I could not resist trying it. So I waited until late at night, then put on my swimming trunks and walked there. I was hoping to be alone, but there were two women already sitting towards the front. I could not really see them through the hot steam, but I heard their voices as they laughed and talked. Determined to enjoy the refreshing, healing steam I entered and stood in the far back of the steam house. I was the only one wearing a swimsuit. I envied their natural freedom and apparent sense of ease. One woman in particular had a very contagious laugh and what seemed to be a very positive attitude about life. After awhile they left together and I was alone. I spent some time in there that night asking God to help me discern the future.

Eight years later, still as pastor of the Forest Grove United Methodist Church, I had joined a few community organizations. One of the retired pastors of the church did the same. He was very active in the community and sometimes forgot to tell people he was the *retired* pastor. This is how I met Deborah for the second time and for the first time formally. The local Chamber of Commerce was concerned about gangs, and Deborah, a member of the chamber, agreed to work on a task force. She hoped to do some positive things for the kids in town. Deborah came into my office at church because she had met the retired pastor, who had neglected to tell her he was retired. She was actually looking for him. She was surprised to meet me, instead. We talked for a short time, and she told me about her work with the Chamber of Commerce. I was already working on some ideas about the needs of youth in our town, so we agreed to meet again to discuss materials from the chamber and see if we could work together. I liked her positive approach to problem solving. We began working together on ideas for positive activities for the local youth. We worked on this project for over a year together during a difficult personal time, as my marriage ended and I once again debated leaving the ministry. In some ways, working on this project, and a few other things I was involved with in the community, functioned as a respite from all the changes happening in my life.

One day Deborah told me she was a licensed Massage Therapist and had attended a class at a hot springs retreat about eight years previously. It was the same hot springs retreat center I had visited that same year. As we continued to talk, and look more closely at one another, it dawned upon us that Deborah was one of the women in the steam house that night! She remembered me, she said, because I was the only man around who wore swimming trunks in the steam room, and she had felt sad because of what she presumed were inhibitions about nudity. At the time, I barely knew Deborah so I was certainly not going to tell her why I felt more comfortable wearing trunks, but it was one more experience where not being free to share my story constricted the conversation.

After our work on the chamber project closed, we continued to meet sometimes for coffee. I enjoyed these conversations, as they generally covered everything from sharing personal faith stories and theological discussion, and current topics of interest in each of our lives to brainstorming practical ideas for community events or art projects. Because of a research project in which Deborah was involved, she began asking me questions about the history of the church's position regarding gay and lesbian, and also intersex, people. We had many in-depth conversations about the long and varied history of LGTBQ people in relationship to the church. We talked about Joan of Arc, who was executed by burning at the stake as much for being transgender and refusing to accept a traditional gender identity as a woman as for any other reason. The church stated that her wearing of male clothing and refusal to stop was an affront to God.

Our conversations also covered medical abnormalities at birth, and the many surgeries performed at birth in operating rooms that determined the declared sex of a newborn when the genitalia was unclear. We read about intersex individuals, and the research that looked into the effects of hormone levels experienced during embryonic development on sexual orientation, and gender identity. These conversations eventually proceeded to include a discussion about transgender people. I began to experience anxiety and torment inside. I desired authenticity; I valued our friendship and I wanted to talk about my history and life from this perspective with someone, after so many years of withholding it. I spent a lot of time in prayer, asking what to do. It had been thirteen years since I had shared this part of myself with another person, but all the same feelings and fears of rejection came rushing back. Eileen was the last person I had told, and that was long before our engagement. After some initial conversations, we rarely mentioned it. I had no idea how Deborah would respond. I was fearful of rejection because Deborah had become a close friend, and I cherished our relationship and shared sense of spirituality. But the topic arose enough times that I knew I had to make some decision. Finally, over coffee one morning, in response to a question, I told Deborah that I was transgender. This led to an ongoing conversation. This conversation is how we began walking in from the wilderness together and I don't expect it will ever end. The outcome of our conversations can be seen in the way we live and express our lives today.

Our friendship grew into courtship and I proposed to Deborah. She accepted, and I gave her an emerald ring. It was deep green, representing new life. We chose May 18, 1996, for our wedding. It was a very joyful occasion. All of our children were present. My mother and many of Deborah's family members were present. Our friends came to celebrate with us. The wedding was held in the church where I was pastor, and many members and friends of the congregation attended as well. Our new lives together began that morning with these vows: "David and Deborah, is it your decision to work together side by side, as your lives are joined together in marriage? Do both of you promise to give yourselves as a source of friendship, companionship, and love? Do both of you promise to keep an open and compassionate mind? Do both of you intend to give of yourselves completely so that all of your days on earth will be a joy to live?" We boldly said yes.

7

Out of the Closet and Into the Streets

I wrap my fear around me like a blanket;
I sailed my ship of safety till I sank it; I'm crawling on your shore.

—"Closer to Fine" by Emily Saliers and The Indigo Girls

Even on our honeymoon Deborah and I talked about our hopes for the future and working together in the church. Our dreams certainly included the desire to help create fully inclusive local churches, and a fully inclusive denomination. We believed that through sharing the gospel and the proclamation of God's love for all persons as evidenced and proclaimed by Jesus, life and ministry would naturally flow in this direction. Returning home to Forest Grove, however, we met our first obstacles. They came in the form of a few parishioners and the retired pastor's opinion about my divorce and remarriage. Although most of the congregation had attended our wedding and celebrated the love and faith we shared, there were a few who believed a divorced person, especially a clergy, should not remarry. While they were a small group, they caused problems by spreading their opinions to other members of my congregation. A few left to attend other churches. This controversy impacted both our personal lives, and our hopes for ministry in that community. It also made it difficult when, on the weekends, our children were home. My son told me that some of the kids at church commented or asked questions about the divorce. This was painful to hear. Going through the divorce had been a difficult time for everyone; it was hard to believe people would want to continue causing stress over a complex issue they knew little about. That is exactly what some people did, though, and so after another year we knew it was pointless to try to work in that community. I asked to move. This time I was not at all sure I wanted to remain in local church ministry. Our family was deeply wounded by what happened in Forest Grove, and my children had already grown to dislike the church in general. Deborah and I had recently moved my mother in with us, and leaving the church would mean another move for her also, and her health was fragile. As a compromise, and to give myself time to think about all of this, I accepted a one-year part-time position as the youth pastor of a larger United Methodist congregation in the Portland area in July 1999. To earn a full-time salary I also worked part-time in a homeless shelter and part-time as a walking messenger in downtown Portland.

The year turned out to be a good experience in the church and for our family. With my mother living with us, our children had an opportunity to get to know their grandmother in a way they never had before. The year also provided an equally important time to reflect on the future. In my daily life, one of the issues and standing jokes was that I had no office. During the course of that year we wrestled about how to solve this problem, but nothing worked. At one point things were so desperate I was given use of a literal closet: it was large enough for a small desk and computer, but it was in the church nursery. This did not work well because it was often in use and unavailable to me. During the short time I tried to use this closet for my office, I found a pin-on button that read, "Out of the closet and into the streets." I wore it to work as a joke about my space in the church, but I also wore it as I knew the time for moving out of my particular closet was approaching on the horizon. The most significant event of that year was taking the youth group and a group of adult chaperones on a mission trip to Glide Memorial United Methodist Church.

Glide is a unique United Methodist church. Located in the Tenderloin district of San Francisco, the church exists among the poor, homeless, LGTBQ, and other communities. Under the leadership of the Rev. Cecil B. Williams, the congregation claimed these communities as their parish and began proactive ministries. Today, the church serves thousands of meals to the hungry each week, provides hygiene kits and medical care to many seniors, manages a low-income and transitional housing program, and welcomes everybody into the life and ministry of the congregation. On a typical Sunday morning, people line up around the block to attend worship, and you can find the wealthy and the well-known worshiping side by side with someone who lives on the street. Our time there with the youth group and other adult chaperones was great, and Deborah and I returned home more hopeful about the church.

I moved back into full-time local church ministry in 2000. The Montavilla United Methodist Church was located in an area filled with opportunities for ministry and outreach. The congregation to which we moved had a reputation of being hard on their pastors, and the person I was replacing had left under duress. Still, I was interested in the congregation, partly as a result of our recent trip to Glide Memorial United Methodist Church. I was anticipating a good and progressive ministry there for several reasons. I had liked meeting members of the congregation, and it seemed there was energy for building an inclusive outreach ministry. There was also an openly gay organist and music director, Don, whom many in the congregation loved. I looked forward to getting to know Don and his partner, who also attended the church. Don loved the United Methodist Church. He had grown up in the church and felt a serious calling to ordained ministry. During my years at Montavilla I watched Don struggle with our denomination's official policy, which forbade the ordination of "self-avowed, practicing homosexuals." Following the 2004 General Conference, when the church upheld this policy yet again, Don could bear it no longer. He had been following his path toward ordination and wanted to be ordained in the United Methodist Church, but in order to fulfill his calling he had to leave the denomination, which he did. Don moved his membership and candidacy for ministry to an inclusive denomination, where he now serves as pastor of a local church. This was truly a loss for the United Methodist Church and one I had come to experience too often over the years.

Montavilla never did become a Portland version of Glide. Perhaps one thing I learned is that no congregation is called to, or can become, the copy of another. But we did accomplish some positive things together during my seven years. Partly as a result of the Disciple Bible Study program I facilitated at Montavilla, many people became increasingly interested in the connection between Christian discipleship, mission, and community outreach. This led to several local community projects and a few trips away. At home, small changes, like replacing our church coffee with a fair trade variety, reflected a growing awareness of the connection between what we profess and what we practice. Our Sunday school wanted to make a positive difference in the community also, and they created kits containing non-perishable food and hygiene items for people in need. Deborah had learned about prayer shawl ministry on the Internet and brought the idea to members of the church. A group in our congregation formed a prayer shawl ministry, and I was blessed to often deliver these gifts. That ministry continued to expand, and a group from church decided to attend the 2006 United Methodist Women's national assembly in Anaheim, California. Women and men from all over the world attended this quadrennial event. We had heard that the assembly would include a display of thousands of prayer shawls created by people from all over the country. We had also formed a worship band at Montavilla, and we were interested in experiencing the diverse styles of music and worship that would be presented. A total of twenty-three women and men from our congregation made the journey together, and it was an inspiring, informative, and incredibly uplifting event. We heard from many talented and dedicated people. We had the opportunity to converse with people representing ministries and communities from all over the world. The worship services were moving and diverse. There was only one omission: there was no mention of welcome to, or ministry among, the LGTBQ community. Although this was nothing new at United Methodist events, this time, as social justice and human rights were lifted up for so many, the absence of recognizing the needs, gifts, and worth of LGTBQ people was painfully noticeable. This was a blot on the whole event for me.

Two of the speakers Deborah and I most looked forward to hearing were a father and daughter, Grammy award-winning musician Emily Saliers and her father, Dr. Don E. Saliers, a distinguished professor of theology and worship at Candler School of Theology. Prior to the assembly, a conservative group in our denomination launched a protest of their appearance because of Emily Salier's sexual orientation. A long clash ensued. In the end, we were able to enjoy their awesome presentation about life, music, and worship. But knowing how my church had insulted and hurt this family moved me another step toward sharing my story. Deborah and I talked about what had happened to the Saliers, and we decided then to explore the best way to tell my history to our grown children, and to my church, both local and denominational.

While I always thought I wanted to wait until our youngest daughter was graduated from college, we knew she was mature enough for this conversation. However, before we could tell any of them, one of our sons came to us with a request. He was friends with a family who had a transgendered child. The child was seven years old and already insisted on being viewed as different from the parents' assigned biological gender. He wondered if I might talk to them or have some resources for them. That event sparked an initial conversation about me. Conversations with our other children followed quickly and positively. At the same time, Deborah and I discussed the process for telling the church.

We prayed about how to move forward. Because I had experienced the contempt, ridicule and misunderstanding that came along with being transgender, I wanted to be certain Deborah understood how much life could change. These conversations and prayers continued until, and after, August 30, 2009. The experience was analogous to being strapped into a roller coaster ride, inching your way to the top of the first hill, knowing you are moving closer and closer to the apex and point of no return. Still, our prayers and conversations continued to move us onward. The logical first step was to meet with my bishop, Bishop Hoshibata. He would be affected by my decision, as would my colleagues. I had told a few close friends and colleagues by this time, including the retired bishop who, without knowing my story, had ordained me in 1982. Everyone agreed it was important to speak with the bishop, and so I made an appointment.

When I went to his office the day of our appointment, I took along the rough draft of a manuscript I began writing following the 2004 General Conference. My intention then was to write something about my life as a transgender United Methodist clergy that I would self-publish to hand out myself at the 2008 General Conference. We opened with prayer and then I shared my history as briefly and succinctly as possible. I tried to be as calm and collected as possible, but I knew I sounded and appeared nervous. Everything seemed a blur as I tried to describe my life as a transgender person, and twenty-seven years as a transgender clergy living within the United Methodist Church. Bishop Hoshibata was very gracious and attentive, asking a few questions for clarification. He was clear that our current *Book of Discipline* contained no restrictions or prohibitions regarding the ordination of transgender persons; he was also clear there was no guarantee about the future. As we completed our meeting, I left him a copy of my manuscript, and we agreed to meet again. We agreed that I would keep him informed of any future plans either for the book or of my circumstances becoming more public. We closed in prayer, and I left feeling that I had done the right thing. I also left realizing that sharing my story and manuscript might complicate our working relationship in the future.

Two months following this meeting, Deborah and I attended a Welcoming Congregation's Conference that focused specifically on transgender persons and the Christian faith. Ironically, the event was held at the same church in Corvallis, Oregon in which I had preached "The Little Ease" the day we voted to become a Reconciling Congregation a decade earlier. This conference was my first immersion into contemporary transgender culture, and a lot had changed. The Internet now made finding other transgender people much easier. It also made gathering information from all over the world possible. I was astounded to hear about surgeons advertizing and competing for transgender clients. I was also surprised to learn how much more control clients had over their own process, and that there were fewer restrictions in many areas of transition than I experienced. Most of all, I was totally amazed that there were so many other people like me living in Portland, Oregon, and all over the planet. I found the event both exhilarating and provoking, and I left more determined than ever to attempt a conversation with my denomination and world about God's inclusive love and the sacred worth of transgender people.

I wrote, I prayed, and I continued my pastoral work. I received the full support of family and friends. I hoped that I might be able to share my story as a transgender person, and actually continue my ministry within the United Methodist Church rather than be estranged from it.

Amidst this preparation, however, a string of events convinced me that Montavilla was not a good setting in which to share my history. Both formal and informal conversations around issues of inclusivity revealed a wide range of opinions. One very outspoken man, who openly talked of his personal struggle with his sexual orientation over his lifetime, would confront me during our weekly prayer gathering whenever I spoke about anything inclusive of LGTBQ people. Another family had left the church because the organist and his partner were involved in the life of the church. And in the tradition of the United Methodist Church, it was time for me to move again. As always, a move is a bittersweet time. As a congregation we remembered high points like the worship band, the Disciple Bible studies, Family Camp, the trip to Anaheim and so much more. We said good-bye to some dreams, including that of becoming a Reconciling Congregation. During the time when new clergy appointments are planned, I had met with my district superintendent, and I had expressed my hope to move to a Reconciling Congregation. Weeks later, I was stunned when she called to ask me to move to Epworth United Methodist Church, a historically Japanese-American congregation located in Portland, Oregon. Besides the fact I knew nothing about the Japanese culture or language, the move meant a big shift in focus, personal finances, and my hope to pastor a Reconciling Congregation. I could not help but wonder if revealing my history to my bishop and, subsequently my district superintendent and cabinet, affected this decision; a decision that appeared unusual in terms of matching clergy and congregation. It was also an unusual decision given my years of ordained ministry in the annual conference. I was told one reason for this particular move was the belief it would be a safe place to share my history when the time came. I became the pastor at Epworth United Methodist Church on July 1, 2007.

Epworth is an extraordinary place. I will forever be grateful to the many who welcomed Deborah and our family into the congregation, with me as their pastor. My initial year at Epworth was spent learning about the culture, history, and community of Japanese-Americans in Portland. I became steeped in this culture, and my world expanded immeasurably. Most profound among these experiences was our participation in the congregation's annual pilgrimage to Minidoka—the site of one of ten Japanese-American internment camps on U.S. soil. These camps were built and used to restrain and contain Japanese-Americans living in the western United States during World War II. Many members of my congregation were held in these camps during the war. Some were born in the camps. During the three years I was the pastor at Epworth, I learned how deeply this experience had affected them. I felt empathy because of my own experiences of ostracism, suspicion, and rejection. While on my pilgrimage to Minidoka, I realized how difficult it was for many of my parishioners to talk about their experience, but I also saw how important speaking their truth was for healing the individual and the community. During this first pilgrimage, I knew it was time to begin making concrete plans to speak my truth. One of the truths that had been revealed to me at Minidoka, as I watched people weep and laugh, reconnect and tell their stories and share memories, was that the cost of oppression and isolation is too much for any individual or group to bear alone.

Things moved quickly following my visit to Minidoka. As I worked on my manuscript, a new vision emerged. Rather than a protest manuscript, to be distributed at the General Conference, I discovered that I wanted to initiate a different kind of conversation—a conversation rooted in the teachings of Jesus, and described in Martin Buber's *I and Thou.* I wanted to try to express what life is like as a transgender Christian clergyman, and engage other people to hear *one another's* stories. Deborah and I prayed and talked about how to proceed. Our experience at Minidoka with our congregation had impacted us so much it seemed impossible not to tell them first. Knowing I still had a lot of writing to do, and had preparations to make with my bishop and my annual conference, we set a date for August, 2009.

Kairos, God's time, had finally come.

8

Coming Out, Again

ON AUGUST 30, 2009, I stepped onto the pulpit of the Epworth United Methodist Church in Portland, Oregon, and shared my story in worship. Things had been building with our Epworth United Methodist congregation for quite some time. In June, I had traveled to Philadelphia, Pennsylvania, to attend the Eighth Annual Philadelphia Trans-Health Conference. This was a huge step for me because I had also agreed to speak on a panel with three other transgender religious leaders. In addition, my spouse and I were meeting with an adult class at Arch Street United Methodist Church in Philadelphia. These were the first two events where I told my story. Although incredibly anxious at first I discovered a new freedom and empowerment as I participated on the panel, met several other transgender religious leaders, and began talking openly about my journey. I was so amazed and hopeful by all the transgender people, especially other religious leaders and people of faith that I met there, that following this experience I knew the time was right to declare my identity openly to my community, church, and world.

Prior to this trip my wife, Deborah, and I met with an elder couple in my congregation to share my personal history. I did not know how to begin, nor did I know what to expect. We sat drinking tea in my office and I began to tell them my journey as a transgender man. They listened quietly, and following a few moments of silence when I ended, both assured me they were fully supportive and had LGTBQ family members and friends. As my bishop had thought, they believed the congregation would be understanding and supportive. Following this very good meeting, I met with a few other people for their opinion and to plan how to tell the congregation. We decided to do this in early September because this is when people tend to regroup after long summer vacations and other activities that interfere with church attendance.

These plans for early September changed, however, when I unexpectedly became a candidate for an award at the Reconciling Ministries Network's Twenty-fifth Anniversary Convocation taking place over the Labor Day weekend in Estes Park, Colorado. The Reconciling Ministries Network is a movement within the United Methodist Church that advocates for changing the denomination's official stance against LGTBQ persons of faith. It is dedicated to creating an open and inclusive denomination where all persons are welcome, regardless of sexual orientation or gender identity. This movement was formed in response to the 1972 changes made in our *Book of Discipline* forbidding the ordination of gays and lesbians. Initially embraced by a handful of people and congregations, this movement continues growing. When I last inquired, it had grown to over three hundred congregations, eighty-six campus ministries and eighty-five other forms of faith communities. There are also many more churches involved in conversation and education about LGTBQ issues in relation to the church. Despite much pressure and negative press from the conservative movement in our denomination, the Reconciling Ministries Network continues to grow and network with similar movements in other denominations and faith communities to promote justice and equality both within the church and in our society.

Unknown to me, Deborah had requested people nominate me for one of the awards being given at this convocation. The award was called "Voice in the Wilderness" and it was to be awarded to a person or group working for the inclusion of all persons within the life of the United Methodist Church despite little or no support. The official language on the certificate is: "The Voice in the Wilderness takes risks to proclaim the righteousness of inclusion for all people in the church, and stands against injustice in places of isolation." Ironically, I had been working on my manuscript, "In From the Wilderness," for two years. Deborah began soliciting nominations, and the next thing I knew we were attending the convocation with me as one of the candidates. This resulted in a need to change the date of sharing my story with the congregation. We knew that being a nominee would make my name and story public, and I did not want anyone to hear it second-hand. So the date for telling the congregation was moved from September to August 30, just one week before our trip to Colorado.

This change in plans created a flurry of activities. I decided to share my story with the Oregon-Idaho Reconciling Ministries group. Although I had participated in activities with them over the years I had never shared my identity as a transgender clergyman. I fretted and worried for weeks prior to the Reconciling United Methodists meeting on August 15. This anxiety helped me realize how unsafe I still felt in the church, even among a supportive community. When the day arrived and I did share my story with shaking knees and trembling voice, they surrounded me with love, support, and practical help. In preparation for August 30, I found myself in the midst of a crash-course led by a conference communications specialist. Ann Craig from GLAAD, The Gay and Lesbian Alliance Against Defamation, also helped me. She taught me how to handle interviews, create talking points, speak with the media, and weed out requests that bordered on sensationalism. A continuing support group formed among local Reconciling United Methodists, offering prayer and practical support. This was deeply appreciated.

Before telling my congregation, I met with a Japanese-American student journalist serving as an intern for a local Portland paper, the *Portland Tribune*. I shared my history with her on the condition it would not go to press until following the worship service on August 30. It was a very good interview, and she and her employer graciously agreed to keep the story unpublished until that Sunday afternoon.

The days prior to the morning of August 30 were a blur of activities, emotions, and conversations. Friends and relatives who worried about our safety helped us prepare a plan of escape in the event our home became unsafe. Some wanted to go so far as to lend us weapons to protect ourselves. My spouse and I talked long into the night about what to do if uninvited media or other people showed up at our home. We wondered how neighbors would react. We questioned the well-being of our young adult children and our pets, and how best to protect them. In the end, we realized there is only so much that can be done to create security for ourselves or our loved ones, and so after much prayer on the evening of August 29, we fell asleep.

On August 30 the church sanctuary was full. The congregation knew I was working on a manuscript and I had promised to tell them what it was about that Sunday. I had also invited some friends and acquaintances I hoped would attend. There were also a number of people from the Oregon-Idaho Reconciling Ministries movement. The atmosphere was almost festive as the service began. My district superintendent, the Rev. Bonnie Parr Philipson, was there to read a statement from our bishop following my disclosure that stated there is currently nothing in our *Book of Discipline* prohibiting transgender people from serving as clergy in the church. In an earlier meeting with her, we had also planned a fellowship time with the congregation following the service for questions and answers in a less formal setting.

Unknown to me, the elder couple in my congregation with whom I had spoken had been quietly talking to a few other people and families in the church. So when the day finally came, there were a few others who already had at least a hint of what I was going to share about my life. I do not remember much about how things began that morning. We had special music and a prayerful chant offered by a Hawaiian dance group, and I met for a special time with our younger worshipers, as I always do. I felt my anxiety and energy rising as I stood to deliver my message. I titled the morning message, "My Book Report."

EPWORTH UNITED METHODIST CHURCH

The Rev. David Weekley, Pastor
08-30-09
James 1: 17–27

My Book Report

Prayer: May the words of my mouth, and the meditations of all of our hearts be acceptable to you, O God, our Creator, Redeemer, and Sustainer. Amen.

First of all, I want to thank you for being here this morning in worship, and for giving me an opportunity to share a little about my manuscript.

I chose to do this in worship because my manuscript, my story, at its core is a spiritual story; it is a faith journey.

Formally, I have been working on my book for about five years, in reality it has been in process for many more years than this—for more than half a century!

A few months ago someone asked me what my book was about. This has been a difficult question to answer until this morning.

I searched for some concise way to reply and said something about it being about my life, my theology, and my relationship with the United Methodist Church, to which he responded, "Well, that will sell about one hundred copies!"

He may be right about that; in fact my book may never be published.

That is alright, and it is not what is most important.

What *is* important is that today the story of my life and faith journey is shared authentically with you in this house of worship.

It is my response this morning to the Scripture reading from James 1:22: "But be doers of the word and not merely hearers who deceive themselves."

All of us carry early life memories and experiences with us through the years, aspects, dimensions of our lives that form our core.

In our present culture, one aspect of life first named and differentiated is the question of whether a baby or child is a boy or a girl. How that question is answered leads to all sorts of ramifications in life as socialization happens.

The toys we play with, the colors we like, the clothes we wear, our friends, and even though there has been progress, there are still activities and professions that are considered dependent upon our sexual identity.

Most often there is no problem between perceived external gender and that baby or child's spirit and core identity—but this is not always so.

In my case it was not so.

From earliest memory, I saw myself as a boy. The boy who would grow into the man you see here today.

My fantasies were about being a football hero, or someone like Zorro, or a military hero.

My friends were other boys on the street. We played baseball, kick-the-can, football, and other games. We built clubhouses by the frog pond.

When I was about five years old I discovered my older brother's discarded First Holy Communion Suit. It fit perfectly and I really liked wearing it, so much so that my parents turned it into my Halloween costume that fall so they could get rid of it.

So, one of my very earliest, formative memories and experiences is me as a little boy.

At first this was no problem, but when I entered public school and kindergarten everything changed, because when the world looked at me, heard my name and talked to my family, they saw a little girl.

As you can imagine, things only worsened as I grew older.

By third grade it was clear I did not fit my assigned gender, and did not fit in a culture that had little or no reference to my experience.

≈ ≈ ≈

Another early, formative memory and experience that forms and informs who I am today is my love of God, and sense of being loved, and connected.

My older brother's First Communion suit was special to me because I knew Communion had to do with Church. When I was little, Bishop Fulton Sheen had a program on television every week, and I used to love watching it.

There was something about his whole personhood that made me feel close to the Jesus he spoke about and told stories of in his messages.

The love of Christ he personified for me carried over into other parts of my life. I used to line up my stuffed animals in my bedroom, open one of my storybooks, and "preach" to them. I wish I could remember what I said.

I do remember sitting outside on summer days when I was nine or ten with our family Bible, trying to read it from beginning to end! And I recall I never made it past Genesis that year! But I also loved sitting outside and talking to God. It's not that I heard some literal voice speaking back, but I always felt a connection and a guiding presence, even as a very young child.

So, my two *earliest* memories and formative experiences in life were:

1. I am a little boy, who is different in some way from other boys and from other people.

2. I am loved by God, and I love God.

These internal truths are what sustained me during all that was to come.

In addition, I was blessed in my life by several adults and peers who saw me through what became a truly horrific adolescence and early young adulthood as many people, peer groups, and institutions tried to force me into an identity I could never own.

Again and again in my life, when things seemed hopeless or at an end, grace intervened.

Two examples stand out for me today. The first took place when I was fifteen years old.

I was at a friend's house and, as I walked into the kitchen, I heard his mom on the telephone talking about a woman named Christine Jorgenson; as I listened, I learned she had not always been seen as a woman, but had been born a male.

She had undergone what was then called sex-reassignment surgery in Denmark.

There was a new hope born in me that day.

As I listened quietly to the conversation, with rising hope I realized that if she could find medical help, so could I. So, at the age of fifteen I determined I would begin to save money to travel to Denmark to obtain medical help to become the whole person, the whole man I understood myself to be.

From the moment I first heard this conversation, grace seemed to intervene at the right moments.

A family friend connected me with their family physician. A trusted teacher in my high school helped me find other supportive adults to talk to about my experience.

When I told my parents, my older brother, and my grandfather they not only were supportive, but they expressed relief to finally know how to help me.

Finally, when the time was right, I made a phone call about where I might go to find medical help for a transgender person.

The answer that came back the next day stunned me: I did not even need to leave my own city. There was a medical team for transgender persons at the University Hospitals in Cleveland, Ohio.

I began meeting with a medical team there in 1972; I was twenty-one years old.

For the next three years I worked with this team, completing every necessary medical, psychiatric, psychological, and socialization test necessary for transgender surgery.

This included beginning hormone therapy, changing legal documents, finding a job and living as a man for a full year before any consideration of surgery.

I did all of these things, and in 1974 and 1975 I underwent a series of surgeries to help make my external gender match my internal one as a man.

The night before my first surgery I prayed a prayer of both thankfulness and intercession to God from my hospital bed, and I fell asleep at peace . . .

~ ~ ~

In 1992, I preached a sermon at First United Methodist Church in Corvallis, Oregon. It was the day that the congregation voted to officially become a Reconciling Congregation, which, in the United Methodist Church, defines a church that is intentionally welcoming to gay, lesbian, bisexual, and transgender people.

In the early part of the message, I shared a true story from my life for the first time.

No one there knew it was about me personally, but it still felt good to stand in the pulpit and speak a part of my hidden truth. This is what I shared that day:

~ ~ ~

It had become a ritual by the time I was in high school. I would get off the bus, enter my house, and go directly to my room. Then I would throw my books on a chair, pound the walls with my fists and cry- cry asking God, "Why?" and then asking God to help me,

*to change me; to make me whole, lovable, and able to share my love
for others openly, like my friends could. I never thought about going
to the Church. Distant memories of the church were of judgment
and condemnation for people like me. The church never seemed to
offer anything caring, or helpful, or hopeful. Years later, when I first
shared my story with a United Methodist clergy, I remember how
my heart was pounding so hard and so fast I thought it was audible
all through the room, like "The Telltale Heart" in the classic story by
Edgar Allen Poe. It was a relief then to be accepted by someone who
was an "official" minister in the church. I did not know then about
all of the other "officials" who felt driven to keep people like me out
of "their" church. Only later did I learn of Lay and Clergy delegates
obsessed with making ever more restrictive changes in* The Book of
Discipline *and in the thinking of Christians everywhere to make certain
people like me could never offer our ministry, our talents; never
share our gifts and unique perspective, our hearts and lives, within
the United Methodist Church.*

～ ～ ～

In that message, I was able for the first time, to connect in public,
my life journey as a transgender man with my faith journey as a
disciple of Jesus.

There were many years that elapsed between my earliest love of
God as a child, and the message I preached in Corvallis in 1992.

There are many years that have passed between that message
of 1992 and our service here today.

Only a few weeks ago, as I shared my story with a member of
the congregation as I made preparations for today, that person said
to me, "Well, it would be a lot easier if you were a plumber."

I agree. But the Spirit moves in mysterious ways.

When I became a member of the United Methodist Church
while I was a graduate student in Oxford, Ohio, I had no idea it
would lead to ordained ministry.

I was working on an academic degree and planning to teach Comparative World Religions.

One day during my prayers, I felt led to explore a vocation in the church.

And although I could not see myself in any public role, or leading worship and speaking in front of a congregation, I still sensed a need to search this direction, so I did enroll in the School of Theology at Boston University.

No one there knew my story, and while I was a student there I learned how unsafe a transgender candidate for ordained ministry was. And so I prayed again and over the weeks decided I would continue to see where seminary led.

When it did lead me into ordained ministry and in the local church, I made a commitment to become the best pastor possible, to serve congregations for as many years as possible, and then to share my story when I felt called to do so. I thought that if I interacted with as many persons as I could, and they experienced me as a good person and pastor, it might be a positive example and witness.

I hoped that by knowing a transgender clergyman personally, many people and congregations would really live up to the current slogan of our denomination and become "open hearts, open minds, open doors" towards those perceived as so different from themselves.

≈ ≈ ≈

These past twenty-seven years have been a true blessing, and I look forward to many more years of ministry.

While serving in a variety of settings and among diverse communities of people, I have been privileged to work in many ministries, preaching the good news of God's love for all persons expressed in and through Jesus the Christ.

During these years I added one more truth to the two I embraced early in my life, so my life experience now taught me three things:

1. I am a little boy who in some ways is different from other boys, and from other people.

2. I am loved by God, and I love God.

3. Most people are different from most other people in some way.

My plan to continue ministry in this hidden way changed dramatically when I went on the Minidoka Pilgrimage with many of you in 2008.

Walking through Minidoka with you I heard many stories, and I learned new words and phrases that resonated within my soul:

Shikata ga nai: it cannot be helped.

Gaman: bearing the unbearable with dignity and grace.

Gambatte: never give up, go for it!

These were words, concepts, tools, and practices to which I could relate; these were experiences with which I felt a kindred spirit.

As I listened to stories at Minidoka, as tears were sometimes shed, and laughter as well, I saw the healing and the understanding that comes through sharing our stories, our authentic and deepest selves.

There is a profound spiritual and emotional healing that can only come to us as we are willing to share our stories and our authentic selves in community.

Again and again, during our Minidoka journey I heard people express the powerful cleansing and sense of freedom they experienced as they shared their personal stories of the internment, sometimes for the first time in over sixty years.

The personal freeing was dramatic, but I also realized the importance of sharing personal stories in order to correct misinformation, and to educate people about the truth through the sharing of personal experience.

Speaking our truth is one powerful way to help end misunderstanding, misinformation, and the abuse that can come when people do not understand those different from themselves. This is one way to be doers of God's word.

Today I pray for this same healing and freedom for each one of us here, as we move to a new level of community together, and as we become comfortable with these basic truths:

1. We love God and God loves us.

2. We are all different from most other people in some way.

3. We still love God, and God still loves us.

◦◦◦◦◦◦

Thank you for listening to my book report; you have become part of the heart of my manuscript.

Shikata ga nai: some things cannot be helped.

But we may practice gaman together, and bear what seems unbearable with dignity and grace; and together, may we always live in the spirit of Gambatte, going for broke wherever God leads us in Christ's name.

In Christ's name.

Amen!

◦◦◦◦◦◦

When I finished delivering the message, the congregation broke into applause. My district superintendent read the statement of support from Bishop Hoshibata. Following the service many hugged me, and Deborah, and thanked me for telling my story. We moved downstairs for a time of refreshments and less formal conversation. Finally, I went back into the sanctuary with a journalist from the *Oregonian*. When Deborah and I finally returned home that day, it was after 4:30 p.m. We were nervous about going home; not knowing what might meet us there. Thankfully everything looked normal, and so we began to relax. But around five o'clock that afternoon we heard a knock on the door and there stood a television reporter and film crew. We politely and firmly closed the door, as we were unprepared to talk with them at that time. I called the station and thanked them for their interest and promised to meet with them at a later date, which I did. That afternoon, both newspapers, the *Portland Tribune* and the *Oregonian* posted my story online. Within hours, our phone was ringing off the hook.

Life has not slowed down since. To date, we have appeared on CBS's, "The Early Show," and declined several offers for television interviews we thought sounded more sensationalist than educational. I have done several radio interviews and local speaking engagements on college campuses and for advocacy and support groups such as PFLAG (Parents and Friends of Lesbians and Gays). Most rewarding and encouraging so far, however, are the letters, cards, emails, and calls I have received describing how sharing this story is giving other LGTBQ people courage to make personal decisions in their lives and to share their truth with others.

I attended my first clergy gathering since my public disclosure at our Bishop's Symposium in October 2009. I was really nervous. It was the first time I would see many of my colleagues together in one place. I did not know what to expect. My overall experience was positive, though there were some who avoided speaking to me or sitting close by. So far as I know, there have been no attempts to bring charges against me. I believe this is largely due to our bishop's public statement to the press, in which he was clear there are no provisions in our *Book of Discipline* to bring me to church trial. How the future will unfold, especially when General Conference meets again in 2012, is anybody's guess. My hope and prayer is that my decision to come in from the wilderness will have a positive impact in the church, and will help lead our denomination and the church universal to live out the gospel mandate to love one another as Christ loves us. The gospel proclaims that God is love and Christ loves us all equally. There are no exceptions. I also hope that sharing my story will be one more piece in helping to educate people about the reality and nature of LGTBQ persons, and the very real continuum along which we all have a place in terms of sexual orientation and gender identity.

Today I depend upon the same grace as John Wesley; and as the composer of Psalm 139: 17–18 declares:

"How weighty to me are your thoughts, O God! How vast is the sum of them!

I try to count them—they are more than the sand;

I come to the end—I am still with you."

At one speaking engagement recently, I was asked if I thought living in this wilderness for twenty-seven years has been worth it. Without hesitation I answered in the affirmative. If my life as a transgender person can make a positive impact on the attitudes of our church and society; if my story encourages one other person, then it is worth everything.

9

The Terror of Breaking Silence in the Church

JULY 1, 2008, began my second year at Epworth United Methodist Church. The year started quietly enough. I was feeling more relaxed than I had in years. Not only was I more familiar both with Japanese culture and my congregation, but I was working hard on my manuscript. One of my favorite sayings around the church came from a man who worked in a local mortuary. We worked together several times while I was pastor of this congregation. He often responded to the pressures we sometimes experienced meeting the needs and schedules of a family planning a funeral or memorial service by saying to me, "No problem, sensei!" (*sensei* is a Japanese word meaning respected teacher). I used this expression of his as a kind of half-humorous mantra while continuing to engage in daily life and ministry knowing that my life would change in the near future. At the same time that my local church grew more familiar, my denomination grew less so. I returned from the Minidoka trip with my congregation more troubled than ever about remaining silent. So many stories were shared on that journey! On the bus, at meals, and at the internment camp itself, people shared their stories, and I saw how much it mattered both to those who spoke and to the ones who listened. I saw that it made a difference, and I learned how much of a difference the willingness to tell personal stories made in the formal reparation and apology made to the Japanese-Americans held in the camps. This experience compelled me to push forward with the process of my own "coming in from the wilderness."

The Japanese-American community officially came in from this wilderness experience of isolation and social marginalization with the passage of the Civil Liberties Act of 1988 and legislation that acknowledged the internment was the result of racial prejudice, war hysteria, and a failure of political leadership. Returning from Minidoka, I wondered about how much prejudice, hysteria, and failure of political leadership continues to imprison thousands of LGTBQ people behind invisible walls, fences, and ceilings.

The 2008 General Conference did nothing to improve the United Methodist Church's recognition of the need to reexamine prejudicial policies. The United Methodist Church certainly did not apologize to LGTBQ Christians, nor did it welcome us as spiritual seekers and leaders into the full life of the church, nor did it rewrite our *Book of Discipline* to reflect either the gospel of Jesus, or the grace-centered theology of John Wesley. The United Methodist Church continues to officially reject LGTBQ people, refusing to include us at the table, or to consider our ecclesiastical and civil rights worthy of protection.

One popular United Methodist author and speaker, the Rev. Adam Hamilton, is considered sensitive towards LGTBQ people. Still, in the most recent edition of his book, *Confronting the Controversies,* he basically rephrases our denomination's traditional view and official stance regarding LGTBQ people. In the chapter devoted to this topic, the Rev. Hamilton says he knows there may be a couple of hundred LGTBQ people in his congregation. He also says he loves them very much and welcomes them each Sunday. At the same time, he places LGTBQ people in a category labeled, "defective" and compares us with children born with spina bifida or Down syndrome.[1] Throughout the chapter, he insists that being born gay or lesbian is not God's ideal and falls short of what God desires for people. However, he admits he does have imperfect vision and knowledge, seeing only through a mirror dimly; as do we all. While the postscript of Hamilton's book

1. Hamilton, *Confronting the Controversies,* 147.

does reveal honest and deep prayer and reflection, this continued categorization of LGTBQ people as being somehow "flawed" and, therefore, of less value than other people is hurtful and harmful. It is a view that leads directly to persecution and abuse.

In contrast to the Rev. Hamilton's concept of gender identity and sexual orientation, psychotherapist David J. Kundtz and consultant Dr. Barnard Schlager note:[2]

> We do not assume that sexual orientation and gender identity are conscious decisions that one makes at a certain point in life . . . Our assumption here is that for the vast number of LGBTQ people, who they are as gendered and sexual beings is an unchangeable given, as it is for heterosexual people.
>
> The analysis of *why* any of us are the way we are will continue for generations, maybe forever . . . The assumption/belief/opinion that LGBTQ people should try to change their sexual orientation or gender to conform with what is seen as "acceptable" is itself one of the most serious problems they face.

Conservative Christians today continue to lobby against LGTBQ persons, refusing to listen to our experience or consider the findings of historical and medical research. Many claim the necessary "treatment" for both sexual orientation and gender identity is a spiritual one, and they offer a number of "faith-based" behavior modification programs to "help" LGTBQ people learn how to live normal lives. None of these programs promise to change a person's sexual orientation or gender identity. Even the authors of these programs know this is not possible. The programs do promise, however, to show LGTBQ people how to suppress their authentic orientation or gender identity in order to fit within current cultural norms.

There has been, and continues to be, horrific abuse of LGTBQ people at the hands of the Christians who run these programs. One of the people who helped encourage me in the second "coming out" journey is the gifted playwright and performer Peterson Toscano. I met Peterson shortly after viewing his play

2. Kundtz and Schlager, *Ministry Among God's Queer Folk,* 7.

Transfigurations: Transgressing Gender in the Bible, which depicts several transgender or gender-non-conforming biblical characters. I went to a production of this one-person performance and was both deeply moved and totally captivated. At this production, I also learned of Peterson Toscano's earlier play, *Doin' Time in the Homo-No-Mo Halfway House.* This is the story of Peterson's own attempts to change his sexual orientation through Christian reparative therapy programs. With poignant stories and characters, he describes the hellish years spent in one Christian therapy program after another, attempting to repress his identity as a gay man. Peterson Toscano put himself through these programs for seventeen years, spending more than thirty thousand dollars. He traveled to three continents before coming to peace with himself and God, finally accepting himself as a beloved child of the God who created him to be exactly who he is.

As the secular world continues to engage in thoughtful conversation about human sexuality and gender identity, many in my denomination would prefer we discontinue any conversation about these issues.

There are many people who would rescind or withhold our civil and human rights. When President Obama openly welcomed LGTBQ people into his campaign, and later appointed a transgender woman, Amanda Simpson, as senior technical advisor to the Commerce Department's Bureau of Industry and Security, some religious conservatives claimed transsexuals should not be hired or given equal protection. In accepting her appointment Simpson stated: "I'm truly honored to have received this appointment and am eager and excited about this opportunity that is before me. And at the same time, as one of the first transgender presidential appointees to the federal government, I hope that I will soon be one of hundreds, and that this appointment opens future opportunities for many others."

Christian Broadcasting Network's David Brody had this to say: "You've got to hand it to the President on this one. He delivered on his campaign slogan because this is definitely 'change you can believe in.' Oy-vey. Someone hand me the Advil. I wonder how this is going to play in the heartland."

Ugly statements like this continue to be voiced daily, and the abuse of LGTBQ persons continues all over the world, sometimes at the hands of government, and too often leading to physical violence, imprisonment, or execution. Too many young LGTBQ people commit suicide as a result of the bullying and abuse presently allowed and tolerated in our society. Still, I trust God with whatever the future holds. To this point, I believe I have been authentic to what I felt called to be and to do. David Brody and the Christian Broadcasting Network certainly do not speak for or represent all Christians. I am a Christian. And I would be remiss not to mention faithful and courageous denominations such as the Metropolitan Community Church, the Evangelical Lutheran Church in America, the United Church of Christ, the Unity Church of Christ, the Unitarian Universalist, as well as organizations that have stood and struggled for an inclusive church within oppressive denominations. Within the United Methodist Church there is Reconciling United Methodists; in other denominations there are groups such as More Light Presbyterians, Episcopal integrity, Roman Catholic Dignity, and Extraordinary Lutheran Ministries all working for full inclusivity. There is also more progressive theological and biblical scholarship represented by a stronger voice in the church today. These are all signs of hope. They are pieces of the puzzle of why I have remained all these years.

I also remain in the church because I love God, and believe in my call to ordained ministry. Like the pastor who first welcomed me into membership in the United Methodist Church back in Oxford, Ohio, I cannot imagine doing anything else than what I do. However, since the early 1980s, our denomination in the United States has experienced a continuous decline in membership. This is also noticeable in most mainline denominations such as my own. I am saddened by what I see and experience. I agree with much of what church leaders have to say regarding healthy and vital congregations, but there is one factor conspicuously missing from the analysis. This factor is the effect of the church's policy regarding LGTBQ people. It continues to oppress people it should welcome, and to support policies and programs of exclusion, which it should oppose. The church is in decline because it refuses to embrace the full inclusivity and hospitality of the gospel. While conservatives claim the church is in decline as a judgment against liberalism and those who welcome LGTBQ persons into the church, I offer the opposite idea: the church is in decline because the verdict is upon those who oppress, and upon those who do not speak up and reach out to the oppressed. In the United States, the oppressed clearly includes LGTBQ people. In an in-depth study that focuses on why people, especially young people, are leaving the church or never enter, David Kinnaman and Gabe Lyons[3] offer six broad reasons why people leave or stay away. The first three have everything to do with the perceived relationship between Christians and the LGTBQ community:

1. *Hypocritical.* Outsiders consider us hypocritical—saying one thing and doing another—and they are skeptical of our morally superior attitudes. They say Christians pretend to be something unreal, conveying a polished image that is not accurate.

2. *Too focused on getting converts.* Outsiders wonder if we genuinely care about them. They feel like targets rather than people. They question our motives when we try to help them "get saved," despite the fact that many of them have already "tried" Jesus and experienced church before.

3. *Anti-homosexual.* Outsiders say that Christians are bigoted and show disdain for gays and lesbians. They say Christians are fixated on curing homosexuals and leveraging political solutions against them.

3. Kinnaan and Lyons, *unchristian,* 29.

As someone who stands both within the institution of the church officially and yet remains an outsider in many critical ways, I believe these defined reasons for church decline accurately reflect social perceptions. Recently discussing this duality of experience with friends, I noted my thoughts about the common experience of imprisonment and rejection shared by the Nisei Japanese-Americans (and LGTBQ people like me), who attempt to live in the church and in society while carrying the scars of personal history from the past, and unsure how people around them see them in the present. A comment was made to me, "Yes, because you were in prison, too." To which I replied, "Yes, that's true. It is also true that I am still in prison. It is only the walls and conditions that have changed. My prison used to be experienced primarily as physical, and it was hell. Today my prison is largely cultural, and while more bearable in significant ways, life today is a paradoxical mix of hell and heaven."

Gaining the insights of the Minidoka experience, and the let down of yet another General Conference, I had an increased urgency to write and to reach out, to reveal my story as one means of contributing to the many voices working to educate and advocate for the rights of LGTBQ people in both secular and sacred space. It is difficult to imagine a more selected, discounted, and rejected group in our nation and world today than the LGTBQ community. Even within *this* community it is well known that gay and lesbian persons do not always include or support transgender people. As one transgender woman expressed, "Maybe it's because compared to us, they seem normal. So they don't want to associate with us." What a sad, self-deprecating comment. For whatever reasons, the fact remains that transgender people are not always, or fully, welcome in the gay and lesbian communities.

In 2009, during a House Subcommittee Health, Education, Labor, and Pensions hearing on transgender rights, this comment was made by Glen Lavy[4] of the Alliance Defense Fund: "Forcing

4. *Transactive Education and Advocacy Newsflash,* June 26, 2008.

people with Christian beliefs to treat transgender as a valid concept is like forcing an orthodox Jew to eat pork." He made the comment following this opening statement by Rep. Tammy Baldwin (D-WI): "There are thousands of transgender Americans who lead incredibly successful, stable lives. They're dedicated parents and they contribute immeasurably to their communities and to their country. Despite these successes hate crimes against transgender Americans are tragically common, and, of course, the focus of today's Hearing, in trying to provide for themselves and their families."

The walls of a social prison shift constantly. They are difficult to perceive until you are in one. I think one reason transgender people sometimes feel so isolated and uncertain of how to reach out is a result of these invisible yet obvious walls. A CNN.com article,[5] "I am transgender, and I want my voice to be heard," describes the personal experience of Rebecca Avery. Always feeling different, at the age of thirteen Rebecca first heard the word that explained her feelings; she was transgender. Currently transitioned and thirty years of age, Rebecca spoke about the difficulties of finding work, additional stress of job interviews as a transgender person, and the spotty protection of the law. For example, she stated that Illinois is one of only thirteen states with a policy protecting transgender people against hiring bias: "The laws help protect me from getting fired or thrown out of my apartment, but they do not help me obtain a career, medical insurance, or housing."

In an ideal world, being transgender would not raise an eyebrow. In the early years following my transition I really did not think of it as an issue. It was only as I lived in the world and observed the attitudes and listened to the assumptions expressed right in front of me that I really began to understand how little other people knew, or perhaps could even imagine what it is like to be lesbian, gay, transgender, bisexual or queer trying to live in the church and in the world. It was not always such a contentious thing, to be a transgender person. Records and artifacts dating as

5. Sarver, "I am transgender," para. 6.

far back as the third millennium BCE illustrate transgender people serving as shamans, sages, and seers. The presence and prevalence of transgender people throughout human history is rich. Unfortunately, my own culture and church do not view transgender people from this perspective. Far from being an ideal world, this is a time and a culture in which LGTBQ people have to seek places for community, safety, support, and spirituality.

I do not think it coincidental that I first shared my story as a transgender man, and a United Methodist clergyman, in a church named Epworth United Methodist Church. John Wesley's father, Samuel Wesley was the pastor at Epworth Church in England. While there, the rectory burned to the ground, and, at the age of five, John Wesley was saved from the flames. This event made a deep impression on his mind, and he said that he regarded himself as one providentially set apart, as a "brand plucked from the burning," quoting Zechariah 3:2. Years later John Wesley came to preach, teach, and rely upon what he described as God's prevenient grace: an unconditional love, an "I-Thou" relationship that nothing can alter. From my earliest memory, my life has been sustained by God's grace. I know I could not have said it like this as a young child, however; I experienced a caring presence that I came to express as God. In times of peace and hopefulness, in times of terror and despair, I have grown to depend upon what I call the presence and the persistence of God.

Addendum: The Little Ease

A sermon preached at First United Methodist Church of Corvallis, Oregon on September 20, 1992, by the Rev. David Weekley Scriptures: Genesis 19:1–11, John 13:31–35

I WOULD like to begin my sermon this morning with a story, or actually, it may not be a story so much as a memory shared by someone about what adolescence was like:

> It had become a ritual by the time I was in high school. I would get off the bus, enter my house, and go directly to my room. Then I would throw my books on the chair, pound the walls with my fists and cry, cry asking God " why?" and asking God to help me, to change me, to make me whole, lovable, and able to share my love openly, like my friends. I never thought about going to the church. Memories of the church were of judgment and condemnation for people like me. The church never seemed to offer anything caring, or helpful, or hopeful. Years later, when I first shared my identity with a United Methodist pastor, I remember how my heart was beating so hard and so fast I thought it could be heard all over the building, like "The Telltale Heart" in that story by Edgar Allen Poe. It was a relief then to be accepted by someone who was an "official" of the church. I did not know then about all the other "officials" who felt driven to keep people like me out of "their" church. Only later did I learn about lay delegates and clergy who were obsessed with making changes in *The Book of Discipline* and in the hearts of Christians everywhere to make certain people like me could never offer our ministry, our talents, or share our gifts, our partners, our lives within The United Methodist Church . . .
>
> I still pray to God. But now I don't pray for God to change me, but to change them. Sometimes I wonder why it is so difficult for people to understand that I am just like them in

virtually every way but one. Why is it so difficult for people to understand that I am just as committed to my family relationships as they are to theirs? Is it *really* that difficult to understand how I feel?

Apparently the answer to this person's questions is "yes, it *is* that difficult." Ballot initiatives in Maine, Colorado, and Oregon are designed to deny homosexuals the protection of civil rights laws, and to mandate that teachers, and other professionals, label homosexual as "perverse, abnormal, and sick."

Our own denominations conservative faction known as the Good News Movement" keeps watch on clergy and bishops who attempt to minister in accepting ways to gay and lesbian Christians, waiting to bring charges based upon their narrow interpretation of *The Book of Discipline.* Christians opposed to social equality, civil rights, and church participation for gays and lesbians always appeal to scripture passages to defend their position. They claim scripture is very clear on this matter, and then selectively cite passages they claim support their views. They accuse Christians who disagree with them of distorting other scripture texts that conflict with their own views.

In a recent New York Times article by Peter Gomes, an American Baptist Minister and professor of Christian Morals at Harvard University, he cites research conducted by Bette Greene. In preparation for a novel Ms. Greene interviewed 400 young men jailed for gay-bashing. In an interview published in the Boston Globe this spring, Greene said she found the gay-bashers generally saw nothing wrong in what they did. More often than not, they said their religious leaders and traditions sanctioned their behavior. One convicted teenage basher told her, the pastor of her church had said, "Homosexuals represent the devil, Satan."

And then Jerry Falwell echoed the same charge. To date, Rev. Pat Robertson has contributed twenty thousand dollars to the Oregon Citizens Alliance to help promote Ballot Measure 9, which would discriminate against gay and lesbian people.

As Peter Gomes states in his article, there are nine biblical passages usually cited by conservative Christians as relating to homosexuality in a condemnatory way. Four of these passages, found in the Old Testament books of Deuteronomy and First and Second Kings, simply forbid prostitution by both women and men. Two other passages, from the book of Leviticus, are part of what scholars define as "The Holiness Code." While this code does ban same-sex activities, it also equally forbids eating raw meat, planting more than one kind of seed in a field, wearing garments made with a blend of fabrics, tattoos, and allowing menstruating women to visit in your home. There are also three references from the New Testament, all attributed to Paul, also cited as referring to homosexuality. In each case it is clear that Paul was concerned with same-sex acts only because in the Greco-Roman culture of his day it represented both the participation in ritual prostitution and the secular sensuality that ran contrary to his view of Jewish-Christian spirituality. As Peter Gomes mentions, Paul was against lust and sensuality in *anyone*, including heterosexuals:

> To say that homosexuality is bad because homosexuals are tempted to do morally doubtful things is to say that heterosexuality is bad because heterosexuals are likewise tempted. For Paul anyone who puts his or her interest ahead of God's is condemned.

This debate over what the Bible may or may not say about homosexuality is not new. For centuries Christian scholars have debated over interpretation of the scriptures regarding homosexuality, as well as many other issues. This morning I will focus on one passage often used to justify the condemnation of homosexuality. This story is found in the nineteenth chapter of the book of Genesis. As I begin, I invite you to reflect upon a few questions about how you understand the interpretation of scripture:

1. What authority does the Bible have in your life?

2. Do you attempt to read every passage in the Bible literally?

3. When you read the Bible do you consider such things as information about the social and cultural climate of biblical times, current scholarship and knowledge, the traditions of our denomination, and your own life experience?

If you follow John Wesley's method of biblical interpretation, you probably consider all of these aspects in your own study of the scriptures. Keeping this in mind, let's look at the nineteenth chapter of Genesis.

One of the most frequently cited passages in the Bible said to condemn homosexuality is the well-known story of Sodom. We all know the story. Two angels came to Sodom and were invited into Lot's home to be his guests for the night. After sharing a meal with his guests, Lot is called outside by the men of the city, young and old, who had surrounded Lot's house. They called out to Lot saying, "Where are the men who came to you tonight? Bring them out to us, so that we may know them." Lot begged them not to act wickedly, and to take his daughters instead, but the men persisted, coming up to Lot's door. Lot's guests pulled him back inside to safety. Because of their actions, the angels of the Lord (Lot's guests) struck the men blind and set in motion the destruction of the city, saving only Lot and his family.

In a careful reading of this story, it is clear that the sin of Sodom had nothing to do with loving, faithful relationships-either homosexual or heterosexual. Many biblical scholars believe the sin for which Sodom was destroyed was the inhospitality with which the men threatened the strangers.

Jewish tradition heavily stressed the ethical treatment of strangers as guests and the men of Sodom clearly broke this ethical code. As one member of our congregation said, hospitality in those days was not just tea and cookies. In biblical times a person's very life often depended upon hospitality, upon being sheltered from the dangers of the night, wildlife, crime, and violence in addition to simply food and shelter. This is the hospitality Lot offered to the men in his house. The story tells us the men of the city demanded to "get acquainted with" the strangers in their midst. Fearing these strangers, these men may well have intended to attack and abuse the foreigners, subjecting them to hostile and violent actions. This is what Lot protects them from experiencing. The most problematic verse is verse five, where one of the Hebrew words for "to know" is used: "Bring them out to us, so that we may know them: But the word used here for "knowing" is *not* the Hebrew term that sometimes has a sexual meaning. Out of 943 uses in the Old Testament, only 10 refer specifically to sexual relations; and even then, only to relations between a husband and a wife. Edward Bauman, in a publication titled, "Reflections on the Gay Life" writes: "The usual word for sexual relationships is not used in this verse . . . what the men of Sodom were demanding was the right' to get acquainted with' the strangers. Clearly, this desire to get acquainted contained an intention to violently humiliate the guests, and Lot protected them in keeping with Jewish ethical customs. This would have been an act of violence, not homosexuality. In the rest of the Bible, and specifically in the gospel of Matthew when Jesus mentions Sodom, the sin of this city is described as inhospitality, and is never referred to as homosexuality:

> And if anyone will not receive you, or listen to your words, shake off the dust from your feet as you leave that town or house. Truly I say to you, it shall be more tolerant on the day of judgment for the land of Sodom and Gomorrah than for that town. (Matthew 10:14–15)

The concept of sexual orientation simply did not exist in biblical times. In the New Testament, Paul does condemn specific acts as prostitution and as part of pagan ritual, but not a homosexual orientation. Two final notes about the New Testament give some clue to early Christian attitudes toward homosexuality: First, Jesus never said one word about homosexuality, even though research has established that ten percent of any population at any time is gay or lesbian. Second, in the entire Bible only six brief passages could be construed as relating to the subject of homosexuality.

There are more scripture passages devoted to dietary laws than to the whole subject of homosexuality. Clearly, this subject was not a significant issue for the early church.

If it is true that homosexuality as an orientation was not even a concept in New Testament times, and if the Bible spends very little time or energy addressing homosexual acts, then perhaps we need to look at church tradition to discover how this issue has become what Peter Gomes refers to as "the last respectable prejudice of this century." Let's begin with Jesus. Jesus did a lot to change many social customs and norms of his own day. For example, we know he shocked and angered people by openly talking with women and including them among his disciples. He also was known for eating with "tax collectors" and other assorted sinners of those times. Jesus challenged injustices and oppression by his living example, and through his teaching and commandment to love one another. (John 13:34–35) Nowhere in the gospels do we find anything to lead us to believe Jesus would have condemned homosexual persons. His basic message was love: unconditional love, the kind of love Jesus taught that God has for every person. It is this love that Jesus both offers and commands: "I give you a new commandment. That you love one another, just as I have loved you, you also should love one another, by this everyone will know that you are my disciples, if you have love for one another."

There can be no question that during his earthly ministry Jesus placed love centrally in his teaching. The gospel of Mark illustrates this central theme in chapter 12:28–34:

> And one of the scribes came up and heard them disputing with one another, and seeing that he answered them well, asked him, ". . . which commandment is the first of all?" Jesus answered: "The first is this, 'Hear O Israel, the Lord is our God. The Lord is One, and you shall love the Lord your God with all your heart and soul and mind and with all you strength.' The second is this, 'You shall love your neighbor as yourself.' There is no other commandment greater than these."

And we all know Jesus' response when asked, "Exactly who is my neighbor?" Remember the story of the Good Samaritan? We know Samaritans were enemies and outcasts—sinners hated by upstanding religious folk; yet Jesus taught that Samaritans were good too, and worthy of God's love just like anybody else. This is what we know Jesus lived, and taught; so, what did the Church do with this simple, basic teaching?

John Boswell states in *Christianity, Social Tolerance, and Homosexuality* that there is no evidence the early Church made a point of opposing homosexuality. The middle ages, however, produced a more pronounced hostility toward homosexuals. Interestingly, this growing intolerance coincides with the growth of the Church as a mainstream economic and political power. This negative attitude toward homosexuals first appeared in popular literature and eventually spread to theological and legal writings. This increasing punitive attitude toward homosexuals was matched by an attitude of intolerance toward all minority groups that increased during the thirteenth and fourteenth centuries. During the middle ages, homosexuals were often burned at the stake. This is likely the origin of the term "faggot," which is still a term of derision today.

The church of the middle ages traditionally condemned homosexuality as unnatural, based upon the premise proposed by Thomas Aquinas that the primary purpose of sexual intercourse is procreation. Intercourse for any other reason is sinful. Since homosexual relationships could not lead to procreation, they were regarded as sinful and unacceptable. This attitude of Western Christian tradition continued to dominate in Europe for the next five hundred years, including the period in which John Wesley lived and worked. Currently, there appears to be no written information about the attitude of early Methodism toward homosexuals. John Wesley never referred to it in any of his teaching or writings. But we do know that Wesley considered the world (and presumably everyone in it) as his parish; and he was known for reaching out in concrete ministries to the powerless and outcast of his own time. He taught his followers to do likewise.

More recently in our United Methodist tradition, there has been and continues to be a split between those who want to keep the homosexual community outside the walls of the church unless they change and those who recognize sexual orientation as a given, a given which includes homosexuality as well as heterosexuality.

As this split has led to legislative struggles on the floor of General Conference, those who want to include gay and lesbian people in the life of the church have formed the "Reconciling Congregation Program." This program allows local churches and church agencies to declare their openness to the full participation of gay men and lesbian women in the church. Currently, there are fifty-four Reconciling churches and four Reconciling Annual Conferences in our denomination. We presently have two Reconciling Congregations in our Annual Conference: the Estacada United Methodist Church and the Metanoia Peace Community. To date, there are several churches engaged in study of this issue in our Annual Conference. In 1988 the Oregon-Idaho Board of Church and Society voted to become a Reconciling Board; and in 1990 the General Commission on Christian Unity and Interreligious Concerns became the first General Reconciling commission of the United Methodist Church. So, our tradition regarding the issue of homosexuality is a varied one. But the message of Jesus and the early church clearly was one of acceptance to all who would follow Jesus. But human judgments, over time, changed this gospel of unconditional love. We might pause here to recall that the Methodist Church once segregated its members by race, and the denomination officially split over the issue of slavery for fifty years. We also have a history of denying women the opportunity to serve as delegates and ordained-clergy, drawing upon Paul's teaching that women are to remain silent in the church. The Bible can be, and has been, interpreted to uphold these views, too. But the United Methodist Church has become more open and inclusive. It no longer condones slavery of any form in any place, and it includes women in all areas of ministry. Our church has changed its stand on these issues, and, in this sense, our tradition gives us hope for the future.

Hope for the future comes from areas outside the church also. Wesley taught his followers to use their heads, to pay attention to the scholarship, and research new discoveries of their day. In the area of human sexuality we continue to learn more all the time. This means we also learn more about homosexuality as one dimension of human sexuality. We know that about ten percent of any population at any time is exclusively homosexual; this is about the same percentage as people who are left-handed, another supposed abnormality once thought to be a sign of God's disfavor, and associated with demonic tendencies!

We also know homosexuality is not a mental illness. In 1973 the American Psychiatric Association voted unanimously to remove homosexuality from its list of mental illness, declaring that it does not constitute a psychiatric disorder, although the stigma and intolerance homosexuals face may lead to emotional distress requiring counseling. The American Psychological Association soon took a similar stand. We also know that homosexuality is a natural phenomenon, occurring in every species of animal in every part of the world. Homosexuality appears in all cultures in every period of time, and social norms have little effect on whether or not homosexual orientations emerge. Homosexual behavior is sometimes tolerated, and sometimes condemned and punished. One of the most pressing questions for many people is: what causes a person to be homosexual? This is a question with virtually no universally accepted answer, though current research leans toward biological and genetic roots. Lesbians and gay men come from all walks of life, and from all types of family backgrounds. Some people say homosexuality is a "lifestyle" and "a choice", but current facts appear to refute this claim; homosexual persons say their same-sex preference is something they discovered and became aware of over time, not a choice they made. The choice they do have, however, is whether or not to be open about their identity and feelings; and it is this issue of sharing identity and feelings that, more than anything else leads me to believe becoming a Reconciling Congregation is the right thing to do.

We have a printed statement on the back of our worship bulletin which reads, "All persons are welcome in this community of faith." As I recall the process through which this statement was added to the bulletin, I remember discussions centered on God's love for us and Jesus' message calling us to love others. We are able to love only because of Christ's love. Because God loves us, we are able to be hospitable to the stranger—protecting and offering shelter from those who would do harm. This is how I understand the words printed on our bulletin. Still, when homosexuality is the issue, it pushes the matter of welcome and hospitality to new horizons for many people in society, and in the church. Some people wonder why a special invitation should be made to people who are homosexual; and some say that a person's sexual orientation is a private matter, not something to make a public issue in either the civil arena or in the church. But who does this silence really protect? Whose comfort level is maintained by this secrecy? In his autobiographical book, *Telling Secrets*, author Frederick Buechner writes, "I not only have my secrets. I *am* my secrets. And you are your secrets . . . Our trusting each other enough to share them with each other has much to do with the secret of what it is to be human."

Certainly there are personal and private areas of our lives that remain "secret" to casual acquaintances and the general public. We all need some degree of privacy and the right to decide how much we allow others to enter into our territory, our life-space. But for most of us, our secrets are selected *by us*, and are composed of relatively specific things about ourselves. What do you suppose life is like for a person whose *entire life* has to be lived in secret, when everything you do and everything you are has to be lived in duplicate: with one face for the office, or family gatherings, and another for your personal life? What do you suppose life is like when your dearest friendships and your committed partnership, which you define as family, and your deepest feelings *all* have to be lived in secret? What is it like when you cannot even discuss openly your personal faith in Christ with fellow Christians because to do so would leave you vulnerable to comments like: "We love you but unless you change you're going to Hell (and I heard that said at a church meeting once) or, "God Hates Gays"? The image that comes to mind is the Tower of London, especially that oldest part of it known as the White Tower, which was built by William the Conqueror in the eleventh Century. On the second floor of the White Tower there is a small Norman Chapel called the Chapel of Saint John. It is very bare and simple. It is built all of stone with twelve stone pillars and a vaulted ceiling. There is a cool silvery light that filters in through the arched windows, and many people express experiencing a sense of peace there, and feeling that they are truly in a holy place. But that is not all there is in the White Tower; directly below the chapel is the most terrible of all the tower's dungeons. It is a dungeon with a heavy oak door that locks out all light and ventilation. It measures only four feet square by four feet high so that a prisoner has no way either to stand upright or to lie down at full length. There is almost no air to breathe in it, almost no room to move; it is known as "the Little Ease."

In many, many ways the Church is the White Tower. At its best the Church is a holy place, a place which brings people closer to God through Christ. At its best, the Church moves in ministries that fulfill Jesus' commandment to love one another—loving one another in the same way and to the same degree God loves us. But we must recognize, too, just how much time and energy the Church has spent, and continues to spend, keeping itself and many of the people who come to it seeking love, in the prison of the Little Ease where there is no ease at all. Imagine being afraid to visit a church, having to wonder if you would be condemned or ostracized on your first visit. That is exactly what many gay and lesbian people fear when they even think about visiting a church; and this fear only increases if they risk becoming active in the church community and making friends there, as many do. They are faced once again with living a divided life, and keeping secret the deepest parts of themselves, wondering: "They accept me now, but what if they find out. Will they still be my friends? Will they reject me and deny all I've given to the congregation?' Will their experience of their church suddenly shift from holy place to the prison of little ease?

A congregation in Southern California conducted a random survey of twelve area churches, calling each one and asking the question: "Would you welcome people who are openly gay or lesbian into your church?" Only one of the churches gave an unequivocal "yes." Two said "no" and hung up. Two referred the callers to another church in the community known to be welcoming and hospitable. The rest of the churches contacted either declined to answer or offered conditions like: "If they are willing to change." Many homosexual people choose not to put themselves through this kind of ordeal, so they have cut themselves off from the Church and all the pain it has brought into their lives. Yet many homosexual people would like to be a part of a Christian community which welcomes them. As a Reconciling Congregation we would identify ourselves as such a place, a place that truly welcomes *all* people, including gay and lesbian people. Other churches that have made this decision have discovered some liberating changes in their congregation. The Rev. Bill Bouton of First United Methodist Church in Oneonta, New York, says: "As a result of becoming a Reconciling Congregation there has been a heightened sense of excitement about *all* of our ministries. And there has been a deepened sense of community. I believe people feel that if we could take the risk of dealing with a human sexuality issue, the other things don't seem so scary."

When congregational members begin, openly and lovingly, to deal with and discuss human sexuality, they break the secrecy that has surrounded one of the most profound elements of human life. They discover that the church and the Gospel of Jesus Christ can bring healing to the most intimate, and sometimes most broken, parts of their lives. But becoming a Reconciling Congregation touches the lives of other people, too. Parents, family members, and friends of gay and lesbian people discover, often for the first time, that it is acceptable to talk about their personal concerns and struggles. Youth struggling with their sexual identity and responsible sexual behavior find positive role models and an openness toward discussion. Nearly all Reconciling Congregations report significant membership growth, even if there has been an initial decline when they made their decision: it seems both homosexual and heterosexual people are attracted to a church that is truly open and welcoming to *all* people. Many congregations report that deeper lines of communication have opened in their community, that members feel a closer bond, and that there is a renewed energy and vitality in their life together.

These positive experiences listed above are all exciting to learn about, but they are not the main reasons I believe a church should become a Reconciling Congregation. The fundamental reason a church should become a Reconciling Congregation is this: Jesus tells us to "Love one another. Just as I have loved you, you also should love one another. By this everyone will know you are my disciples." We are called to become a Reconciling Congregation because of God's love and forgiveness toward us. Because of this love we experience we seek to reflect God's love in our relationships with other people. If we love a person, we do not ask that person to live a double life, a life in which their friendships, their family, their feelings, and their faith must remain a secret. If we love someone, we do not imprison them, we do not place them in the Little Ease where there is no light, no air, no comfort, and rest. We may not fully understand or even agree on questions like the origin of homosexuality. But hopefully, we can agree that because of the love Christ gives to us and asks us simply to give to others, becoming a Reconciling Congregation is the right thing to do. Amen.

Study Guide for

In From The Wilderness, Sherman(She-r-man)

By J. Ann Craig and Rev. David E. Weekley

INTRODUCTION

DAVID AND Deborah Weekley crossed paths with me in that historic moment when the Rev. David Weekley decided to share his story with his congregation. David shared with them that thirty-five years earlier, he had transitioned from female to male.

At the time, I was working for the Gay & Lesbian Alliance Against Defamation (GLAAD) as the first director of the Religion, Faith and Values program. My mission was to help faith leaders use the media to speak publicly in support of the moral equality of lesbian, gay, bisexual and transgender people. So, when I saw an article about David's sermon in a Portland newspaper, I picked up the phone to offer GLAAD's assistance.

Soon, David and Deborah were preparing to be interviewed on the CBS Morning Show. As I helped prepare David and leaders in his congregation to talk to reporters, what everyone agreed on was that David was an outstanding pastor. They did not have to understand everything about being transgender; they just knew that David lived out his love of God and served God's people.

As you read this book, you are probably going to be like most of us. We don't know everything there is to know about gender identity or why some people choose to transition. You can rest easy that you are on the journey with all of us to understand the diversity in God's beloved creation we call "humankind."

Out of this journey a study guide emerged to help readers explore their questions. The study guide will help you talk together as people who also have stories to share. All of us have stories about differences in ourselves, our families, our friends, and our church members. These differences may not be about gender, but they allow us to walk in another person's shoes.

The study guide will give you some of the tools to know more about what it means to be transgender. We will explore the nature of gender itself and how humankind has a wide range of gender expressions and biological differences that don't necessarily fall neatly into "male" and "female."

As Christians, we will delve into the Bible and think about Eve being taken from Adam's rib—a female from a male. We'll talk about Paul saying there is no longer male or female and how gender difference in eunuchs of the Old and New Testament informs our understanding of God's expansive love. We will look at how things are not always as they seem. When Jesus broke the bread and helped the disciples to see things in a new way.

Hopefully, David's and my collaboration will be a tool to help you say out loud that you are learning about transgender people in the church. If you have the opportunity, read this book in a study group or with a Christian friend. The organization of United Methodist Women has approved this book for their 2013 reading program. Mothers and fathers and families whose children are gender non-conforming are waiting for the church tell them that their children are among those who are gathered around Jesus and to be blessed.

David story is a story and this study guide helps us understand the love of Jesus for the whole people of God—not just for those who fit gender expectations.

So, we invite you to relax, open your hands and receive the gift that David is offering—his whole life story.

SESSION 1

Kairos and Awakening: Chapters 1–4

BIBLE STUDY:

Psalms 139: 1–3, 13–14
Genesis 1:27
So God created mankind in his own image,
  in the image of God he created them;
  male and female he created them.

Genesis 2:20–23
But for Adam no suitable helper was found. 21So the LORD God caused the man to fall into a deep sleep; and while he was sleeping, he took one of the man's ribs and then closed up the place with flesh. 22Then the LORD God made a woman from the rib he had taken out of the man, and he brought her to the man. 23The man said, "This is now bone of my bones and flesh of my flesh; she shall be called 'woman,' for she was taken out of man."

REFLECTION

These scriptures are working hard to communicate what it means to be male and female. In both stories, there is a unified gender identity—God is both genders since both male and female are created in God's image. And, in what might be called the first surgical transition to female, God takes a rib from Adam and creates a female.

These stories are usually thought of as God's stamp of approval on gender and reproductive roles, but can we begin to think about these texts as a way to talk about our oneness with God and each other, and how closely we are related to each other in our maleness and femaleness?

God's response to "Men are from Mars and Women are from Venus" is that we are all from God and we all come from each other.

DISCUSSION:

- What does it mean to be "one in Christ"?

- What did Paul mean when he said there is neither male nor female?

- What does the other Genesis story about God creating humankind out of clay say about us?

- What were the gender behavior and identifications then? Now?

- What were the consequences of breaching those expectations then? Now?

DAVID'S STORY: THE BEGINNING AND HIS NEW BEGINNING AS OPENLY TRANSGENDER

Kairos, the first chapter in David's book describes the Sunday morning when he told his story to the congregation. Many people were prepared, but for some it was the first knowledge of David's life as transgender.

Think about your experience of secrets and telling stories of truth.

- Are you a person who people trust with their secrets?

- When is truth telling a growth experience?

- Who were the officials that were brought into the process in David's story?

- What other relationships did he consider when telling his story?

- Reflect on the secrets kept by choice and secrets that are imposed on us.

- Are you a person who people trust with their secrets?

Adults in David's life were brave enough to help him think through his own gender and gender expectations of society.

- Discuss how you learned about gender and gender expectations.

- Have you ever experienced telling a child that they are a girl or they are a boy?

- What does it tell you that a child has to be taught about their gender?

- Have you ever known a child whose expressed gender differs from what you expect?

SESSION 2

Transitioning: Chapters 2–4

BIBLE STUDY:

Matthew 19:12
"For there are eunuchs who were born that way, and there are eunuchs who have been made eunuchs by others—and there are those who choose to live like eunuchs for the sake of the kingdom of heaven. The one who can accept this should accept it."

- What do you think Jesus was saying here?
- Who is he talking about regarding "the one who can accept this should . . ."?
- What roles did eunuchs play in Greco-Roman and Jewish society at that time?

Act 8: 27–39
Phillip was told by the Spirit to go to a specific road and he met an Ethiopian eunuch who, when he believed, asked, "What is to prevent me from being baptized?" The answer to that was "Everything" but Phillip baptized him. He was a foreigner, a eunuch and person of privilege and power—everything that the disciples close to Jesus were not.

DISCUSSION:

- What does this say about who should be included in full baptism and the full participation in the church?
- The early church was transitioning from exclusive rules and beliefs to inclusive sharing of the Gospel of Jesus. What other transitions was the church going through?

- David Weekley transitioned from being female to male—and transitioned into the ministry through his spiritual journey.

- For an interesting study on eunuchs and sexual minorities in the Bible, go to http://epistle.us/hbarticles/eunuchs1.html.

David's Story: Gender Identity, Being Transgender and Transitioning

David provides a moving and insightful description of his experience of realizing that he understood himself to be male, even though he was growing up in a female body.

Exercises:

- Look through the pictures on pages 46–51 looking for the boyishness of David.

- On google, find a random class composite of grade school kids. Discuss the range of gender expression in the children. You can cut a few of their pictures out and, as a group line them up according to how masculine or feminine they are. There are clues about whether they are male or female—hair length and clothing but if you can ignore these clues and just focus in on their faces, you will find that some girls express more masculine traits than some boys.

These traits are both physically and socially defined. For most transgender people, there is a serious disconnect between their inner identity and their physical gender.

David tells his story about having to deal with teachers who target him for extra punishment, other students who bullied and harassed him and administrators who did not defend him for simply being different.

EXERCISE:

- Discuss who taught you and when you were taught about being a boy or a girl. What were the rules that you liked and the rules that were unwanted or difficult? Have you ever been asked by a child if you are a boy or a girl?

DISCUSSION:

- Have you or someone you care about ever been criticized or bullied for being different? If you are comfortable, share a story. If you are in a larger group, break up into pairs to share. Share your story, but if the story is too emotional, set up a time with your pastor or with a counselor to explore your story in a safe and professional environment.

- In talking about gender identity and medical treatments now available, it is first important to use terminology that is appropriate.

EXERCISE:

If you want to make this a learning experience,

- Before you gather as a study group, photocopy the list in enlarged format

- Cut out the words and the definitions;

- Ask the participants to match the definitions with the words.

- What words have you learned previously that are now considered derogatory?

- Who gets to choose which words are offensive? Why?

- Think about your feelings during the exercise.

- Which words are more comfortable?

- Be patient and generous with each other. This may be the first time you have seen some of these words. Read the list over and help each other make the matches.

GENERAL TERMINOLOGY

Sex: The classification of people as male or female. At birth, infants are assigned a sex based on a combination of bodily characteristics including: chromosomes, hormones, internal reproductive organs, and genitals.

Gender Identity: One's internal, personal sense of being a man or a woman (or a boy or girl.) For transgender people, their birth-assigned sex and their own internal sense of gender identity do not match.

Gender Expression: External manifestation of one's gender identity, usually expressed through "masculine," "feminine" or gender variant behavior, clothing, haircut, voice or body characteristics. Typically, transgender people seek to make their gender expression match their gender identity, rather than their birth-assigned sex.

Sexual Orientation: Describes an individual's enduring physical, romantic, emotional and/or spiritual attraction to another person. Gender identity and sexual orientation are not the same. Transgender people may be heterosexual, lesbian, gay, or bisexual. For example, a man who becomes a woman and is attracted to other women would be identified as a lesbian.

TRANSGENDER-SPECIFIC TERMINOLOGY

Transgender: An umbrella term for people whose gender identity and/or gender expression differs from the sex they were assigned at birth. The term may include but is not limited to: transsexuals, cross-dressers, and other gender-variant people. Transgender people may identify as female-to-male (FTM) or male-to-female (MTF). Use the descriptive term (*transgender, transsexual, cross-dresser,* FTM or MTF) preferred by the individual. Transgender people may or may not choose to alter their bodies hormonally and/or surgically.

Transsexual (also Transexual): An older term which originated in the medical and psychological communities. Many transgender people prefer the term "transgender" to "transsexual." Some transsexual people still prefer to use the term to describe themselves. However, unlike *transgender, transsexual* is not an umbrella term, and many transgender people do not identify as transsexual. It is best to ask which term an individual prefers.

Transvestite: DEROGATORY see *Cross-Dressing*

Transition: Altering one's birth sex is not a one-step procedure; it is a complex process that occurs over a long period of time. Transition includes some or all of the following cultural, legal and medical adjustments: telling one's family, friends, and/or co-workers; changing one's name and/or sex on legal documents; hormone therapy; and possibly (though not always) some form of surgical alteration.

Sex Reassignment Surgery (SRS): Refers to surgical alteration, and is only one small part of transition (see *Transition* above). This term is preferred rather than "sex change operation." Not all transgender people choose to or can afford to have SRS. Journalists should avoid overemphasizing the importance of SRS to the transition process.

Cross-Dressing: To occasionally wear clothes traditionally associated with people of the other sex. Cross-dressers are usually comfortable with the sex they were assigned at birth and do not wish to change. **"Cross-dresser" should NOT be used to describe someone who has transitioned to live full-time as the other sex, or who intends to do so in the future.** Cross-dressing is a form of gender expression and is not necessarily tied to erotic activity. Cross-dressing is not indicative of sexual orientation.

Gender Identity Disorder (GID): A controversial DSM-IV diagnosis given to transgender and other gender-variant people. Because it labels people as "disordered," Gender Identity Disorder is often considered offensive. The diagnosis is frequently given to children who don't conform to expected gender norms in terms of dress, play or behavior. Such children are often subjected to intense psychotherapy, behavior modification and/or institutionalization. This term replaces the outdated term "gender dysphoria."

Intersex: Describing a person whose biological sex is ambiguous. There are many genetic, hormonal or anatomical variations which make a person's sex ambiguous (i.e., Klinefelter Syndrome, Adrenal Hyperplasia). Parents and medical professionals often assign intersex infants a sex and perform surgical operations to conform the infant's body to that assignment. This practice has become increasingly controversial as intersex adults are speaking out against the practice, accusing doctors of genital mutilation.

TRANSGENDER TERMINOLOGY TO AVOID

Problematic Terminology

PROBLEMATIC: "transgenders," "a transgender"
PREFERRED: "transgender people," "a transgender person"
Transgender should be used as an adjective, not as a noun. Do not say, "Tony is a transgender," or "The parade included many

transgenders." Instead say, "Tony is a transgender person," or
"The parade included many transgender people."

PROBLEMATIC: "transgendered"
PREFERRED: "transgender"
The word transgender never needs the extraneous "ed" at the end
of the word. In fact, such a construction is grammatically incor-
rect. Only verbs can be transformed into participles by adding
"-ed" to the end of the word, and transgender is an adjective, not
a verb.

PROBLEMATIC: "sex change," "pre-operative," "post-operative"
PREFERRED: "transition"
Referring to a sex change operation, or using terms such as
pre- or post-operative, inaccurately suggests that one must have
surgery in order to truly change one's gender.

PROBLEMATIC: "hermaphrodite"
PREFERRED: "intersex person"
The word "hermaphrodite" is an outdated, stigmatizing and mis-
leading word, usually used to sensationalize intersex people.

Defamatory Terminology

Defamatory: "deceptive," "fooling," "pretending," "posing," or
"masquerading"
Gender identity is an integral part of a person's identity. Please do
not characterize transgender people as "deceptive," as "fooling"
other people, or as "pretending" to be, "posing" or "masquerading" as a man or a woman. Such descriptions are extremely
insulting.

Defamatory: "she-male," "he-she," "it," "trannie," "tranny,"
"gender-bender"

These words only serve to dehumanize transgender people and
should not be used (*SeeDefamatory Language*).

NAMES & PRONOUN USAGE

We encourage you to use a transgender person's chosen name.
Often transgender people cannot afford a legal name change or
are not yet old enough to change their name legally. They should
be afforded the same respect for their chosen name as anyone else
who lives by a name other than their birth name (e.g., celebrities).

*We also encourage you to ask transgender people which pronoun
they would like you to use.* A person who identifies as a certain
gender, whether or not they have taken hormones or had surgery,
should be referred to using the pronouns appropriate for that
gender.

*If it is not possible to ask the person which pronoun he or she pre-
fers, use the pronoun that is consistent with the person's appearance
and gender expression.* For example, if the person wears a dress
and uses the name "Susan," feminine pronouns are appropriate.

*It is never appropriate to put quotation marks around either the
transgender person's chosen name or the pronoun that reflects
their gender identity.*

DAVID'S STORY:

People helped David all along the way but for every person who
was supportive, there were others who felt frightened by David
and often tried to hurt him. Friends, family and officials often did
not understand. But a brave teacher asked him about his own comfort with his gender and introduced David to medical people who
had an understanding of transgender people. Even in the medical
world, a few treated him with scorn and even breached health pro-
tocols which could have injured him.

DISCUSSION:

- David had many people who helped him along his journey. What person has done that for you as you discovered who you are?

- How can the church reach out to Transgender people? Here are some facts based on research in Washington D.C.

  - In 2006, the District of Columbia added a provision for "gender identity and gender expression" in its Human Rights Act, and therefore explicitly prohibited discrimination against gender-variant people including the District's transgender community. This population remains, however, marginalized by the discrimination it faces on a daily basis and suffers from being essentially invisible in official data.

  - According to the Washington Transgender Needs Assessment Survey (WTNAS), the District's transgender population has lower educational outcomes with 40% of the respondents without a high school diploma.

  - In fact, employment is the biggest obstacle to overcome for trans people: In the District of Columbia, 42% of respondents were unemployed, 29% had no income and 31% had incomes of under $10,000/year (source: WTNAS).

  - According to the National Transgender Discrimination Survey, 15% of transgender people reported incomes of $10,000 or lower, compared with 7% for the general population.

  - Consequently, housing instability remains an issue: 26% of transgender people have a hard time finding different places to sleep at for short periods of time and 11% have been evicted at least one.

- In the District, 19% of transgender respondents do not have a living space, and 13% of those who have a living space do not feel safe in their own home (source: WTNAS)

Many of us have known people who were told they were not welcome in the church or in church leadership because of who they are.

- Women were long excluded from ministry and to this day are far more underpaid and don't survive being a local church pastor very often.

- African Americans were segregated into the Central Jurisdiction for decades.

- Gay and lesbian United Methodists are blocked from ordination, banned from marriage or blessings, tried in church court and some have been denied membership.

- Transgender pastors have been challenged in church court but have not been officially banned, in spite of efforts at General Conference to implement such policies.

SESSION 3

Into the Wilderness—Into the church

Bible Study:

Engage in a word study on "wilderness" in the New Testament

- Jesus went to the wilderness after his baptism to be tested
- Moses is referred to as leading the Hebrews in the wilderness
- John came from the wilderness.   Jesus went into the wilderness to retreat and pray.

Discussion:

- Why would the church feel like the wilderness to David Weekley?
- What did Jesus learn from being tempted in the wilderness?
- What does David Weekley learn from the wilderness?
- What have your wilderness experiences been? These can be literal or metaphorical.

David's Story: Defending the Disenfranchised

David understood his own story and did not feel free to speak out. Even women who were challenging the gender roles rejected transgender people, some saying they do not exist. But David continued to speak out and helped a congregation in Corvallis, Oregon, explore and embrace the process of becoming a Reconciling Congregation. (See page 112 for the full sermon.)

After the congregation voted to become Reconciling he was unexpectedly transferred. David reflected on whether his advocacy for gay and lesbian Christians was the motivation for the move—but was never sure. His marriage frayed and the silence imposed on him and his wife took its toll. That marriage ended. Years later, with a stalwart belief in God and love and despite a terrible loss with the failure of his first marriage, David and Deborah met, fell in love and married.

Discussion:

- When have you stood up for someone else because you didn't feel like you could speak out about your own issues? Have you seen others do this?

- On page 77 David and Deborah discuss the range of gender identity realities. What were you taught about intersex people? For a detailed and clinical discussion of intersex people Wikipedia is very informative: http://en.wikipedia.org/wiki/Intersex. For more personal discussions, go to http://www.isna.org/faq/what_is_intersex

- How do you determine the church's rules on ordination of gay people and restrictions on marriage when it comes to intersex or transgender people?

- David's first marriage ended but he chose to risk his heart again and married Deborah. Given the range of gender that we have learned about, what would be your feeling if someone you loved, or with whom you were falling in love shared with you that they were transgender.

SESSION 4: BREAKING THE SILENCE

"Coming Out—Again!"

Jesus in the breaking of the bread

Jesus don't tell anyone

The silence of God

"No Problem Sensei!"

When David came out publicly as transgender, he had to think about whether or not he would lose relationships with his congregation, denomination, children, community, and more. After the first flurry of media coverage and conversations in the church, David had to decide if he would continue asking people to think about transgender concerns or just settle in and be a pastor.

EXERCISE:

- Search on Google news archives to read about transgender people in the news. You can look for the articles about David a Deborah and print them out for the group. Make a collection of headlines related to transgender stories.

    - What are the main topics of the headlines?

    - What main points are being made by journalists about transgender people?

- Talk about how secrets function in your life, the life of your family and your church family.

    - Think about the secrets in your extended family. Are their secrets that if told could put family members in the way of harm? Rejection? Violence? Judgment?

- Are there secrets in your extended family that could bring attention—either negative or positive?
- How do secrets function in your church family?
- Is there truth telling that is difficult but could help people live more full and open lives?

- Bring in a few newspapers and magazines.

  - Have people look for and cut out headlines that focus on revealed secrets and revealed truth or facts.

  - Create one or more collages on newsprint.

  - With a marker write a statement about something positive that comes out of the revelations.

Closing Activity:

If possible invite a transgender person or panel of persons in your community to talk with you about their life and experience.

Bibliography

Alexander, Neil M., ed. *The Book of Discipline of the United Methodist Church.* Nashville: United Methodist Publishing, 2008.

Buber, Martin. *I and Thou.* New York: Scribner, 1958.

Chellew-Hodge, Candace. *Bulletproof Faith.* San Francisco: Jossey-Bass, 2008.

DiNovo, Cheri. *Qu(e)erying Evangelism.* Cleveland: Pilgrim, 2005.

Dzmura, Noach. *Balancing on the Mechitza.* Berkeley: North Atlantic, 2010.

Geis, Sally B., and Donald E. Messer. *Caught in the Crossfire.* Nashville: Abingdon, 1994.

Green, Jamison. *Becoming a Visible Man.* Nashville: Vanderbilt University Press, 2004.

Hamilton, Adam. *Confronting the Controversies.* Nashville: Abingdon, 2005.

Hilton, Bruce. *Can Homophobia Be Cured?* Nashville: Abingdon Press, 1992.

Hinnant, Olive Elaine. *God Comes Out.* Cleveland: Pilgrim, 2007.

Jorgensen, Christine. *Christine Jorgensen: A Personal Autobiography.* San Francisco: Cleis, 1967.

Kinnaman, David, and Gabe Lyons. *unchristian.* Grand Rapids: Baker, 2007.

Kundtz, David J., and Bernard S. Schlager. *Ministry Among God's Queer Folk.* Cleveland: Pilgrim, 2007.

Mollenkott, Virginia Ramey. *Omnigender: a trans-religious approach.* Cleveland: Pilgrim, 2001.

———. *Sensuous Spirituality: Out from Fundamentalism.* Cleveland: Pilgrim, 2007.

Mollenkott, Virginia, and Vanessa Sheridan. *Transgender Journeys.* Eugene: Resource Publications, 2010.

Peterson, Eugene H. *The Message.* Colorado Springs: Navpress, 1993.

Sarver, Jordan. "I am transgender, and I want my voice to be heard." Online: http://articles.cnn.com/2010-04-14/living/transgender.irpt_1_transgender-gender-identity-illinois?_s=PM:LIVING.

Tanis, Justin. *Trans-Gendered: Theology of Ministry and Faith Communities.* Cleveland: Pilgrim, 2003.

Waun, Maurine C. *More than Welcome.* St. Louis: Chalice, 1999.